Anti-Inflammato[ry]

COOKBOOK FOR BEGINNERS

REVOLUTIONIZE YOUR HEALTH WITH ALL NATURAL RECIPES

Jaime Campbell© Copyright 2023

All rights reserved.

It is not permitted in any way to reproduce, duplicate, or transmit any part of this document in digital or printed form. Dissemination of this publication is strictly prohibited, and any use of this document is not permitted without the prior written con-sent of the publisher. All rights reserved.

The accuracy and integrity of the information contained herein is guaranteed, but no responsibility of any kind is assumed. It is in fact, in terms of misinterpretation of the information through carelessness, or through the use or misuse of any policies, processes, or instructions contained within the book, the sole and absolute responsibility of the intended reader. Under no circumstances may the publisher be legally prosecuted or blamed for any damage done or monetary loss incurred as a result of information contained in this book, either directly or indirectly.

Rights are held by the respective authors and not the publisher.

Hide these books

Legal Note: This book is copyrighted. It is for personal use only. No part of the contents of this book may be modified, distributed, sold, used, quoted, or paraphrased without the specific consent of the author or copyright owner.

Any violation of these terms will be sanctioned as provided by law.

Disclaimer:

Please note that the contents of this book are exclusively-for educational and entertainment purposes. Every measure has been taken to provide accurate, up-to-date, and completely reliable information. No warranties of any kind are expressed or implied. Readers acknowledge that the author's opinion is not to be substituted for legal, financial, medical, or professional advice.

TABLE OF CONTENTS

Introduction 1
The importance of a balanced diet 2
The benefits of a diet based on 3
Anti-inflammatory foods 3
List of foods to avoid 3
List of foods in general 4
Measurement conversion table 5
Shopping list 5

BREAKFAST RECIPES
Apple porridge 7
Avocado and raspberry toast 8
Berry porridge 9
Scrambled eggs with salmon 10
Yogurt with fruit and cereals 11
Yogurt with peaches and wholemeal biscuits 12

SNACKS RECIPES
Apple, kiwi, and cucumber smoothie 13
Carrot, grapefruit, and ginger smoothie 14
Detox cocktail 15
Frozen yogurt with cherries 16
Masala Chai 17
Whole-grain sandwich with turkey 18

FIRST COURSE RECIPES
Beetroot cream 19
Black rice with avocado and crabmeat 20
Black rice with chicken and vegetables 21
Black rice with salmon 22
Brown rice with chicken and mint 23
Brown rice with zucchini, tuna, and avocado 24
Buddha bowl with black rice and chicken 25
Carrot, spring onion and ginger cream 26
Chilled Cucumber Ginger Soup 27
Cream of asparagus 28
Cream of beans and shrimp 29
Cream of beans, salmon, and celery 30
Cream of broad beans and peas 31
Cream of pumpkin and mushrooms 32
Cream of pumpkin and shrimp 33
Lentil and mushroom soup 34
Mushroom and hazelnut soup 35
Pasta salad with avocado and tuna 36
Pasta salad with green bean cream 37
Pepper and Carrot Soup 38
Poke bowl with shrimp 39
Rice with spinach and salmon 40
Saffron leek cream 41
Spaghetti with shrimp and cherry tomatoes 42
Spaghetti with tuna and pumpkin 43
Spaghetti with zucchini 44
Tomato lentil soup 45
Tomato porridge 46
Tomato soup 47
Whole-wheat pasta with peppers 48
Whole-wheat spaghetti with lemon 49

SECOND COURSE RECIPES
Almond and spice breaded cod 50
Asparagus and vinegar tuna 51
Avocado and grapefruit Alaska Pollock 52
Basil pistachio and turmeric mackerel 53
Broccoli jalapeño tilapia 54
Coconut milk and beets green salmon 55
Ginger and jalapeno baked tuna 56
Asparagus and honey salmon 57
Kale and berries plaice 58
Lettuce and tofu cheese salmon salad 59
Mushroom cream plaice fillet 60
Orange and avocado halibut 61
Pecans and carrot creamy tuna 62
Pineapple turmeric and star anise sea bream 63
Soy cheese and veggies cod 64
Spinach herbs and nuts pangasius 65
Steamed sage and ginger halibut 66
Tangerine and pineapple cod 67
Tilapia with lime and pecans 68
Trout and zucchini fish meatballs 69
Yogurt and mushrooms tuna fillet 70
Zucchini and avocado turmeric salmon 71
Cauliflower chia seeds and ginger chicken 72
Chicken and veggies taste salad 73
Cucumber turkey and grapefruit salad 74
Herbs and melon sauce chicken cubes 75
Garlic and pistachio turkey legs 76
Mango and pineapple and chicken skewers 77
Mustard and seeds chicken thighs 78
Orange turkey and veggies 79
Radicchio and apple chicken salad 80
Sweet and sour turkey with asparagus 81
Yogurt and chives chicken burger 82
Zucchini and mushrooms chicken 83

SIDE DISHES
Avocado and turkey omelette 84
Baked ginger zucchini eggs and soy cheese 85
Carrot and egg white frittata 86
Smoked salmon and chia seeds eggs 87
Spinach and tuna eggs 88
Almond, carrot and red cabbage 89
Asparagus and almond soy salad 90
Radicchio, avocado and cherry tomato salad 91
Baked zucchini and artichokes 92
Coleslaw with mushrooms 93
Green beans and carrots tofu cheese 94
Seeds and nuts stuffed avocado 95
Soy cheese and hazelnuts cucumber rolls 96
Turmeric and coconut spinach 97

28 DAYS MEAL PLAN 98

INTRODUCTION

Welcome to this anti-inflammatory cookbook! This comprehensive beginner's guide is dedicated to this life-changing diet, so you can embrace good health and longevity. As a practical guide, this book aims to help you learn about this diet and apply it to your daily life. Inside, you'll find detailed explanations and advice, along with a mouth-watering collection of recipes and an easy-to-use meal plan.

WHAT IS INFLAMMATION?

Before we begin, it's important to explore what we mean by inflammation. Inflammation (or phlogosis) is a form of damage to the body caused by an excessive immune reaction. The damage doesn't usually destroy cells, but long-lasting (or chronic) inflammation can cause a wide range of major health problems. Inflammation can be caused by physical agents (trauma, heat), chemical agents (acids, etc.), toxic agents, and agents of a biological nature (bacteria, viruses, etc.).

Inflammation is a natural function that's designed to eliminate the underlying threat. It also helps to repair the damage caused to tissues and to restore, through the decisive intervention of defensive cells, the normal functionality of the organism. Based on its duration, inflammation can be divided into two main types:

Acute: When the duration corresponds to only a few days and triggers symptoms that are generally temporary, which disappear when the inflammatory response has been successful, such as a sore throat or itching.

Chronic: When the duration of the inflammation continues over time (and therefore does not disappear within a few days). This can be caused by a defect in the inflammatory response regulation mechanisms, or when the body's ability to remove the harmful agent is compromised.

The most challenging part of inflammation is that it's not always possible to completely eliminate the cause. It's also possible to encounter problems in the healing process. In these cases, chronic inflammation can be generated – the duration and effects of which vary according to the body's ability to heal the damage.

A common example is an allergic reaction. In an allergy, pollen or another irritant (usually harmless to most people) causes a spike in inflammation and a strong autoimmune reaction. Chronic inflammation can also be caused by bacteria or viruses that are capable of resisting the body's immune response, such as certain mushrooms, as well as materials like metal or wood splinters and silica dust.

It's important to understand that inflammation must be removed before it becomes chronic, as it can lead to even more serious consequences for your health. But it's equally important to try to prevent inflammation and, in this case, an anti-inflammatory diet can play an important role in your long-term wellbeing.

THE IMPORTANCE OF A BALANCED DIET

How can we work to prevent chronic inflammation? For this task, it's important to underline the importance of diet. A good diet contains plenty of balanced foods that restore the correct degree of alkalinity in our bodies.

WHY IS ALKALINITY IMPORTANT?

Our bodies are naturally alkaline, and in this condition, inflammation is easier to resolve. But if our pH levels become too acidic, this creates an environment where pathogens and inflammation are pushed into overdrive. The purpose of a balanced diet is therefore to keep the levels of acidity and basicity at their correct levels. An unbalanced diet, especially one high in acidic foods, ends up considerably altering the acid/base balance of our body, which can lead to the loss of essential minerals such as calcium and magnesium.

Under normal conditions, our body keeps the acid/base balance of our body fluids stable. The key to maintaining good health is preserving this internal balance between acids and bases. Our body is precisely designed to maintain a balance between acidity and alkalinity, technically defined as **acid/base balance** or, as it's commonly called, the pH level.

PH is a logarithmic value of concentration that determines the acidic or basic (alkaline) nature of a solution. It's typically displayed as a value between 0 and 14:

- Acid: For values between 0 and 6.9
- Neutral: Equal to 7
- Basic or alkaline: For values between 7.1 and 14

When this balance is compromised, our body runs into numerous problems, including increased levels of inflammation, impaired immune function, and weight gain. An ideal balanced diet should be divided into a ratio of 80% alkalizing and 20% acidifying foods. This acid/base balance is essential to maintain, and it's extremely important if you want to achieve a healthier body and reduce your chances of becoming sick. Breaking it down, an anti-inflammatory diet includes the consumption of:

- 80% alkalizing foods: including vegetables, fresh fruit, fruit juices, tubers, dried fruit, and legumes.
- 20% acidifying foods, trying to greatly limit the consumption of foods such as refined cereals, meats, dairy products, and alcohol.

THE BENEFITS OF A DIET BASED ON ANTI-INFLAMMATORY FOODS

Now that we've discovered the best ratio for promoting a balanced diet, let's delve into the powerful health-boosting effects of anti-inflammatory foods.

A strongly acidic physiological environment predisposes our body to high levels of inflammation, which leads to a lowering of the immune system and a state of general psycho-physical malaise. On the contrary, an alkaline (and therefore anti-inflammatory) body helps to prevent, and in some cases even to cure, many physical ailments and pathologies. Below, you'll discover the most important benefits that you can obtain by following an anti-inflammatory diet:

Counteracts cellular aging. A high intake of fibers, vitamins, minerals, salts, and antioxidants can reduce the effects of cellular oxidation. In particular, the antioxidants contained in foods cancel cellular oxidation, simultaneously slowing down tissue damage.

Helps reduce the risk of developing various diseases and chronic conditions

Helps reduce kidney stones and gout. The reduction of foods that contain inflammatory substances-and more specifically, the reduction of the intake of proteins of animal origin-reduces the risk of developing these two issues.

Helps prevent osteoporosis. Osteoporosis is a progressive bone disease, mainly characterized by the decrease of minerals in the bone tissue. This diet, thanks to the high potassium intake and the low sodium intake, should have a positive effect on your calcium balance and bone health. In this way, the onset of osteoporosis can be prevented, also reducing the risk of fractures in older people.

Helps prevent diabetes. A high acidic pH level causes metabolic damage, reducing the ability of insulin to regulate blood sugar levels. An alkaline diet, limiting the use of excessively refined sugars, can help prevent diabetes.

Helps in the fight against extra pounds. The anti-inflammatory diet is a natural, healthy, and sustainable method for reducing your calorie intake and regaining your physical shape.

It helps to develop muscle mass and consequently prevents cardiovascular diseases.

Helps activate vitamin D, thanks to the increased intracellular concentration of magnesium which acts as a coenzyme.

LIST OF FOODS TO AVOID

So now we've discovered the many surprising health benefits of the anti-inflammatory diet. But which acidic foods cause the most damage to our bodies? Below, you'll find the top foods to avoid when you begin your new anti-inflammatory lifestyle.

These foods should be limited to the maximum because once metabolized, they throw your body's pH balance out of balance and lead to an increase in inflammation. In addition to the foods you'll need to cut out entirely, there are additional foods that, while still acidic, you can safely limit.

All foods that contain sugars are typically considered acidifiers, especially refined, leavened foods, foods that are too refined or chemically treated, foods cooked in the microwave, and fermented or processed foods.
Cereals, except for whole meal ones, all have a strong acidifying power. Foods of animal origin are also pro-inflammatory, especially and red meat. Milk and dairy products should also be avoided as they have a strong acidifying power. Foods with a high inflammatory content are:

Meat (especially red)

Milk and fatty cheeses.

Hydrogenated fats

Coffee

Red wine and alcohol in general

Refined sugar

Refined Cereals

Sausages

Ready-to-eat, packaged and canned foods

LIST OF FOODS IN GENERAL

To make things even easier for you, so that you can fully understand the concept of anti-inflammatory and non-anti-inflammatory foods, here's a list of all foods-including even the very inflammatory ones-divided by category. You'll also find an indication about the degree of acidity (red bar for very inflammatory, orange bar for moderately inflammatory, bar green for those with little inflammation). So, let's begin!

FOODS WITH HIGH INFLAMMATORY POWER

- Beer
- Carbonated and sugary drinks
- Coffee
- Fructose
- Jams
- Ketchup
- Lamb
- Liqueurs
- Mayonnaise
- Pasteurized milk and fatty cheeses
- Peanuts
- Pork meat
- Pumpkin seeds
- Red meat
- Refined grains and baked goods
- Refined white sugar
- Seitan
- Sunflower seeds
- Sweeteners
- Tender
- White rice
- Wine

FOODS WITH MODERATE INFLAMMATORY POWER

- Cashew nuts
- Chestnuts
- Eggs
- Honey
- Legumes
- Light cheeses
- Mustard
- Parsnip
- Potatoes
- Poultry

FOODS WITH HIGH ANTI-INFLAMMATORY POWER (VERY LITTLE OR ZERO INFLAMMATION)

- Agar agar
- Algae
- Almonds
- Amaranth
- Apples
- Apricots
- Asparagus
- Avocado
- Bananas
- Broccoli
- Cabbage
- Carrot
- Celery
- Chili
- Cucumber
- Curry
- Dates
- European bass
- Extracted and centrifuged
- Figs
- Garlic
- Ginger
- Grape
- Green tea
- Herbal teas
- Herbs
- Himalayan salt
- Lemon
- Low-fat white and Greek yogurt
- Mango
- Maracujam, Passion Fruit, Papaya
- Mile
- Onions
- Oranges
- Parsley
- Peaches
- Pears
- Pineapple
- Quinoa
- Raisins
- Salmon
- Soy sauce
- Spinach
- Sprouts
- Tofu and soy cheese
- Trout
- Tuna
- Vegetable milk
- Watermelon
- Zucchini

MEASUREMENT CONVERSION TABLE

WEIGHT CONVERSION TABLE (US Strandard)

½ oz = 14 g	7 oz = 196 g
¾ oz = 21 g	8 oz = 224 g
1 oz = 28 g	9 oz = 252 g
1½ oz = 42 g	10 oz = 280 g
2 oz = 56 g	12 oz = 336 g
2½ oz = 70 g	1 lb = 453 g
3 oz = 84 g	1 lb 8 oz = 677 g
4 oz = 112 g	2 lbs = 906 g
4½ oz = 126 g	3 lbs = 1.36 kg
5 oz = 140 g	1 tbsp = 15 g
6 oz = 168 g	1 tsp = 5

LIQUID CONVERSION TABLE (US Strandard)

- 1 cup = 240 ml
- 1/2 cup = 120 ml
- 1/3 cup = 80 ml
- 1/4 cup = 60 ml
- 1 tablespoon (tbsp) = 15 ml
- 1 teaspoon (tsp) = 5 ml
- 1 fluid ounce = 29 ml
- 1 quart = 0,95 liter

TEMPERATURES EQUIVALENTES (°C Approximate)

- 300 °F = 150 °C
- 325 °F = 160 °C
- 350 °F = 180 °C
- 375 °F = 190 °C
- 400 °F = 205 °C
- 425 °F = 220 °C
- °F = Fahrenheit °C = Celsius

SHOPPING LIST

VEGETABLES

- Artichokes
- Asparagus
- Broad beans
- Broccoli
- Cabbages
- Cannellini beans
- Carrots
- Cauliflowers
- Celeries
- Cherry tomatoes
- Cucumbers
- Green cabbages
- Kale
- Kidney beans
- Leeks
- Lentils (normal, red)
- Lettuce
- Mushrooms (different types)
- Onions (different types)
- Peas
- Peppers
- Pumpkins
- Radicchio
- Red beets
- Salad
- Scallions
- Shallots
- Spinaches
- Spring onions
- Tomatoes
- Zucchinis

FRUITS

- Almonds
- Apples
- Apricots
- Avocado
- Bananas
- Blackberries
- Black olives
- Blueberries
- Cherries
- Figs
- Grapefruits (pink and normal)
- Hazelnuts
- Kiwis
- Lemon
- Limes
- Mangoes
- Melons
- Oranges
- Peaches
- Pears
- Pecan nuts
- Pineapples
- Pistachios
- Raspberries
- Strawberries
- Tangerines
- Walnuts
- Watermelon

MEAT/FISH

- Alaska Pollock
- Chicken
- Cod
- Crabmeat
- Halibut
- Pangasius
- Plaice
- Salmon
- Sea bream
- Shrimp tails
- Smoked salmon
- Tilapia
- Trout
- Tuna
- Turkey

MISCELLANEUS

- Flour (Almond and Soy)
- Spices (cardamom, chili, cinnamon, cloves, curry, fennel seeds, fish mixed spices, garlic, ginger, juniper berries, mustard seed, sweet/smoked paprika, black/green/pink pepper, saffron, star anise, turmeric powder)
- Vinegar (Apple cider and Rice)
- Aromatic plants (basil, bay leaves, dill, chieves, cilantro, oregano, lemongrass, mint, parsley, rosemary, sage, thyme)
- Rice (black and brown)
- Teas (black, green, herbal)
- Chia seeds
- Vegetable Milk (Coconut, unsweetened Almond)
- Dark chocolate
- Pasta (Durum/whole-wheat)
- Eggs
- Stock/broth (fish and vegetables)
- Oil (garlic flavored, olive, extra-vergin olive)
- Yogurt (greek, low fat white)
- Salt (normal and Himalayan)
- Honey
- Jalapeno

Amazing collection of all natural recipes!

Are you ready to begin your anti-inflammatory lifestyle? Here is an amazing collection of quick and easy recipes that you can use to restore your pH balance, revitalize your body, and begin defeating chronic inflammation. All of these recipes include calories and nutritional values (displayed per portion). Every recipe uses grams per portion measurements for calories and macronutrients.

BREAKFAST RECIPES

Apple porridge

PREP. TIME	COOKING TIME	DIFFICULTY	A.I. GRADE
15 minutes	10 minutes	●○○○○	Good

INGREDIENTS FOR 2 SERVINGS

- 2 apples
- 4 tbsp rolled oats
- 10.5 oz of sugar free vegetable milk
- 1 tsp ground cinnamon
- 2 tbsp of chopped almonds

INGREDIENTS FOR 3 SERVINGS

- 3 apples
- 6 tbsp rolled oats
- 16 oz of sugar free vegetable milk
- 2 tsp ground cinnamon
- 3 tbsp of chopped almonds

DIRECTIONS

1. Peel the apples and then grate them.
2. Put the vegetable milk in a saucepan and bring it to a boil.
3. Add the rolled oats, grated apples and cinnamon, and cook for 5 minutes, stirring constantly.
4. Put the porridge in two cups, sprinkle it with the chopped almonds and serve.

NUTRITIONAL VALUES:

CARBS	PROTEINS	FATS	CALORIES
34gr	9gr	10gr	267

BREAKFAST RECIPES

Avocado and raspberry toast

INGREDIENTS FOR 2 SERVINGS

- 2 slices of rye bread
- ½ avocado
- 1 lime
- 2 tbsp fresh raspberries
- Salt to taste

INGREDIENTS FOR 3 SERVINGS

- 3 slices of rye bread
- 1 avocado
- 2 little size limes
- 3 tbsp fresh raspberries
- Salt to taste

PREP. TIME	COOKING TIME	DIFFICULTY	A.I. GRADE
15 minutes	2 minutes	●○○○○	Good

DIRECTIONS

1. Peel the avocado, remove the pulp, and put it in a bowl.
2. Mash the avocado pulp with a fork, add the lime juice and salt and mix well.
3. Place the slices of bread in the toaster and toast them for a couple of minutes, or until crispy
4. Divide the rye bread in half and then spread the avocado on top.
5. Wash and dry the raspberries and place them on top of the toast.
6. Put the toasts on two plates and serve.

NUTRITIONAL VALUES:

CARBS	PROTEINS	FATS	CALORIES
18gr	8gr	11gr	210

BREAKFAST RECIPES

Berry porridge

PREP. TIME	COOKING TIME	DIFFICULTY	A.I. GRADE
15 minutes	20 minutes	●○○○○	Good

INGREDIENTS FOR 2 SERVINGS

- 2.4 oz of rolled oats
- ½ glass of water
- ½ glass of sugar free vegetable milk
- 2 tbsp of honey
- ½ tsp vanilla essence
- 3.5 oz of berries
- 1 tsp of chopped hazelnuts
- ½ banana

INGREDIENTS FOR 3 SERVINGS

- 3.6 oz of rolled oats
- 1 glass of water
- 1 glass of sugar free vegetable milk
- 3 tbsp of honey
- 1 tsp vanilla essence
- 5.7 oz of berries
- 2 tsp of chopped hazelnuts
- 1 banana

DIRECTIONS

1. Put the vegetable milk and water in a saucepan and bring to a boil.
2. Add the oat flakes, honey and vanilla essence and mix well.
3. Cook the porridge for 10 minutes. Bring to a boil and cook for another 5 minutes, stirring constantly.
4. Pour the porridge into two bowls.
5. Wash and dry the berries and put them on the porridge.
6. Peel the banana cut it into slices and put it in the bowls.
7. Finally, add the chopped hazelnuts and serve.

NUTRITIONAL VALUES:

CARBS	PROTEINS	FATS	CALORIES
42gr	13gr	5gr	214

BREAKFAST RECIPES

Scrambled eggs with salmon

INGREDIENTS FOR 2 SERVINGS

- 3 eggs
- 3.5 oz of smoked salmon
- 1 tsp of chopped dill
- 1 tsp chopped chives
- Salt and black pepper to taste
- Olive oil to taste

INGREDIENTS FOR 3 SERVINGS

- 5 eggs
- 5.7 oz of smoked salmon
- 2 tsp of chopped dill
- 2 tsp chopped chives
- Salt and black pepper to taste
- Olive oil to taste

PREP. TIME	COOKING TIME	DIFFICULTY	A.I. GRADE
10 minutes	10 minutes	●○○○○	Top

DIRECTIONS

1. Place the eggs in a bowl and add salt, pepper, and dill.
2. Mix with a fork until you get a homogeneous mixture.
3. Heat a little oil in a pan and, when hot, add the eggs.
4. Cook for 5 minutes, stirring frequently. Eggs should be creamy and soft.
5. Divide the eggs between two plates.
6. Cut the salmon into slices and add it to the eggs.
7. Sprinkle with chives and serve..

NUTRITIONAL VALUES:

CARBS	PROTEINS	FATS	CALORIES
1gr	18gr	10gr	146

BREAKFAST RECIPES

Yogurt with fruit and cereals

**INGREDIENTS
FOR 2 SERVINGS**

- 4.2 oz of Greek yogurt
- 2 tbsp of whole-grains cereals
- 2 tbsp blackberries
- 2 tsp of honeya

**INGREDIENTS
FOR 3 SERVINGS**

- 5.3 oz of Greek yogurt
- 3 tbsp of whole-grains cereals
- 3 tbsp blackberries
- 3 tsp of honey

PREP. TIME	COOKING TIME	DIFFICULTY	A.I. GRADE
10 minutes	/	●○○○○	Good

DIRECTIONS

1. Put the yogurt in a bowl, add the honey and mix well.
2. Chop the cereal and put it in the bottom of two cups.
3. Pour over the yogurt cream and level it with a spoon.
4. Wash the blackberries, dry them, and divide them equally over the yogurt cream.
5. You can serve your yogurt with fruit and cereals.

NUTRITIONAL VALUES:

CARBS	PROTEINS	FATS	CALORIES
9gr	10gr	6gr	150

BREAKFAST RECIPES

Yogurt with peaches and wholemeal biscuits

INGREDIENTS
FOR 2 SERVINGS

- 2 wholemeal biscuits
- 3 ripe peaches
- 1 cup of Greek yogurt
- 2 tsp of honey
- 2 tsp ground cinnamon
- 2 tbsp chopped hazelnuts

INGREDIENTS
FOR 3 SERVINGS

- 3 wholemeal biscuits
- 4 ripe peaches
- 1 cup and ½ of Greek yogurt
- 3 tsp of honey
- 3 tsp ground cinnamon
- 3 tbsp chopped hazelnuts

PREP. TIME	COOKING TIME	DIFFICULTY	A.I. GRADE
15 minutes	/	●○○○○	Good

DIRECTIONS

1. Put the yogurt in a bowl with the honey and cinnamon and mix well.
2. Put the biscuits in the mixer and chop them finely.
3. Peel the peaches and cut them into slices.
4. Take two glass cups and put the crumbled biscuits on the bottom.
5. Then alternate a layer of yogurt with one of the peaches and finish with the yogurt.
6. Sprinkle with chopped hazelnuts and serve.

NUTRITIONAL VALUES:

CARBS	PROTEINS	FATS	CALORIES
19gr	5gr	4gr	128

SNACKS RECIPES

Apple, kiwi, and cucumber smoothie

INGREDIENTS
FOR 2 SERVINGS

- 2 green apples
- 2 cucumbers
- 4 kiwis
- 1 cup of Greek yogurt
- 1 glass of unsweetened almond milk

INGREDIENTS
FOR 3 SERVINGS

- 3 green apples
- 3 cucumbers
- 6 kiwis
- 1 cup and ½ of Greek yogurt
- 1 glass and ½ of unsweetened almond milk

PREP. TIME	COOKING TIME	DIFFICULTY	A.I. GRADE
15 minutes	/	●○○○○	Top

DIRECTIONS

1. Peel the apples, remove the seeds and core, and cut them into small pieces.
2. Wash the cucumbers, peel them, and cut them into cubes.
3. Peel the kiwis and cut them into 4 parts.
4. Put the cucumbers, kiwis, and apples in the blender.
5. Add the yoghurt and almond milk and blend for 1 minute to obtain a creamy smoothie.
6. Divide the smoothie between two glasses and serve.

NUTRITIONAL VALUES:

CARBS	PROTEINS	FATS	CALORIES
17gr	1gr	1gr	75

SNACKS RECIPES

Carrot, grapefruit, and ginger smoothie

INGREDIENTS FOR 2 SERVINGS

- 2 grapefruits
- 4 carrots
- 2 tsp grated fresh ginger
- 2tsp of honey

INGREDIENTS FOR 3 SERVINGS

- 3 grapefruits
- 6 carrots
- 3 tsp grated fresh ginger
- 3 tsp of honey

PREP. TIME	COOKING TIME	DIFFICULTY	A.I. GRADE
10 minutes	/	●○○○○	Top

DIRECTIONS

1. Wash the carrots, peel them, and then grate them.
2. Squeeze the grapefruit juice directly into the blender glass.
3. Add the carrots, honey, and ginger.
4. Activate the blender and blend until the carrots are completely dissolved.
5. Pour the smoothie into two glasses and serve.

NUTRITIONAL VALUES:

CARBS	PROTEINS	FATS	CALORIES
14gr	2gr	2gr	106

SNACKS RECIPES

Detox cocktail

INGREDIENTS FOR 2 SERVINGS

- 4 lemons
- 2 grapefruits
- 1 green apple
- 1 tsp fresh grated ginger
- 2 tsp of honey
- 1 glass of water

INGREDIENTS FOR 3 SERVINGS

- 6 lemons
- 3 grapefruits
- 2 green apple
- 2 tsp fresh grated ginger
- 3 tsp of honey
- 1 cup and 1 tsp of water

PREP. TIME	COOKING TIME	DIFFICULTY	A.I. GRADE
15 minutes	/	●○○○○	Good

DIRECTIONS

1. Peel the apple and cut it into slices.
2. Cut the grapefruit and lemons in half and cut horizontally two round slices from the grapefruit and 6 slices from the lemons. Cut the grapefruit and lemon slices into wedges and put them in a jug.
3. Squeeze the remaining lemons and grapefruits and strain the juice into the jug.
4. Finally add the honey, ginger and glass of water and mix well.
5. Put the cocktail in the fridge and let it cool until it's time to use it.
6. Pour the cocktail into two tall glasses, add a few ice cubes, and serve.

NUTRITIONAL VALUES:

CARBS	PROTEINS	FATS	CALORIES
14gr	1gr	1gr	60

SNACKS RECIPES

Frozen yogurt with cherries

INGREDIENTS FOR 2 SERVINGS

- 8.8 oz of Greek yogurt
- 1.7 oz of sugar free vegetable milk
- 2 tbsp of honey
- 8 pitted cherries
- 1 tbsp 90% dark chocolate, cut into shavings

INGREDIENTS FOR 3 SERVINGS

- 13.2 oz of Greek yogurt
- 2.5 oz of sugar free vegetable milk
- 3 tbsp of honey
- 12 pitted cherries
- 3 tsp 90% dark chocolate, cut into shavings

PREP. TIME	COOKING TIME	DIFFICULTY	A.I. GRADE
20 minutes + 4 hours to rest in the freezer	/	●○○○○	Good

DIRECTIONS

1. Put the yogurt, honey, and milk in a bowl.
2. Take an immersion blender and blend until smooth.
3. Put the mixture in a container with low sides, close it and put it in the freezer.
4. Keep the mixture in the freezer for about 4 hours, taking care to mix it every 30 minutes to break the ice crystals.
5. After 4 hours, take the mixture, divide it into pieces and put it in the blender.
6. Blend for 30 seconds, then turn off the blender and divide the frozen yogurt into two bowls.
7. Add the pitted cherries and chocolate flakes and serve.

NUTRITIONAL VALUES:

CARBS	PROTEINS	FATS	CALORIES
11gr	6gr	4gr	82

SNACKS RECIPES

Masala Chai

INGREDIENTS FOR 2 SERVINGS

- 2 sachets of black tea
- 1 cinnamon stick
- 2 tsp cardamom powder
- 2 cloves
- ½ tsp of fennel seeds
- ½ tsp ground ginger
- 10.5 oz of water
- 4 tbsp of sugar free vegetable milk

INGREDIENTS FOR 3 SERVINGS

- 3 sachets of black tea
- 2 cinnamon stick
- 3 tsp cardamom powder
- 3 cloves
- 1 tsp of fennel seeds
- 1 tsp ground ginger
- 16 oz of water
- 6 tbsp of sugar free vegetable milk

PREP. TIME	COOKING TIME	DIFFICULTY	A.I. GRADE
15 minutes	10 minutes	●○○○○	Top

DIRECTIONS

1. Put the cardamom, cloves and fennel seeds in a mortar and grind them coarsely.
2. Pour the spices into a saucepan with the water and add the ginger and cinnamon.
3. Bring to a boil and boil for 4 minutes.
4. Filter the liquid obtained by pouring it, while it is still boiling, directly into the cups.
5. Add the black tea bag and leave to infuse for 3 minutes.
6. After 3 minutes, remove the tea bags, add the milk, mix well and then serve.

NUTRITIONAL VALUES:

CARBS	PROTEINS	FATS	CALORIES
1gr	1gr	0gr	10

SNACKS RECIPES

Whole-grain sandwich with turkey

**INGREDIENTS
FOR 2 SERVINGS**

- 4 slices of whole-grain sandwich bread
- 4 slices of roasted turkey
- 1 ripe red tomato
- 2 fresh basil leaves

**INGREDIENTS
FOR 3 SERVINGS**

- 6 slices of whole-grain sandwich bread
- 6 slices of roasted turkey
- 2 ripe red tomatoes
- 3 fresh basil leaves

PREP. TIME	COOKING TIME	DIFFICULTY	A.I. GRADE
10 minutes	2 minutes	●○○○○	Good

DIRECTIONS

1. Put the slices of bread in the toaster and let them toast for a couple of minutes.
2. Once ready, place the slices of bread on a cutting board.
3. Wash the tomato and cut it into thin slices.
4. Also, wash the basil leaves.
5. Put the turkey, the tomato and finally the basil on two slices of bread.
6. Close with the other slices of bread, cut them in half, put them on two plates and serve.

NUTRITIONAL VALUES:

CARBS	PROTEINS	FATS	CALORIES
28gr	12gr	6gr	218

FIRST COURSE RECIPES

Beetroot cream

INGREDIENTS FOR 2 SERVINGS

- 10.5 oz of precooked red beets
- 1 carrot
- ½ onion
- 2 cups of vegetable broth
- 2 tbsp of tofu cheese
- 1 tsp chopped chives
- Salt and black pepper to taste
- Olive oil to taste

INGREDIENTS FOR 3 SERVINGS

- 16 oz of precooked red beets
- 2 carrots
- 1 onion
- 3 cups of vegetable broth
- 3 tbsp of tofu cheese
- 2 tsp chopped chives
- Salt and black pepper to taste
- Olive oil to taste

PREP. TIME	COOKING TIME	DIFFICULTY	A.I. GRADE
15 minutes	40 minutes	●●○○○	Good

DIRECTIONS

1. Peel the carrot, wash it, and cut it into pieces.
2. Cut the red beets into small pieces.
3. Heat a drizzle of oil in a saucepan, add the finely chopped onion and let it brown.
4. Add the red beets and carrots and let them cook for a few minutes. Add a ladle of broth and continue cooking for 30 minutes, adding the rest of the broth from time to time.
5. When the vegetables are soft, season them with salt and turn off the heat.
6. Blend the soup obtained with an immersion blender.
7. Divide the cream between two plates, add the tofu cheese and chives and serve.

NUTRITIONAL VALUES:

CARBS	PROTEINS	FATS	CALORIES
19gr	12gr	10gr	221

FIRST COURSE RECIPES

Black rice with avocado and crabmeat

INGREDIENTS FOR 2 SERVINGS

- 5 oz of black rice
- 1 little size avocado
- 3.5 oz cooked crabmeat
- 4 mint leaves
- ½ lemon
- 1 tbsp of olive oil
- Salt and pepper to taste

INGREDIENTS FOR 3 SERVINGS

- 7.5 oz of black rice
- 1 big-size avocado
- 5.7 oz cooked crabmeat
- 6 mint leaves
- 1 lemon
- 2 tbsp of olive oil
- Salt and pepper to taste

PREP. TIME	COOKING TIME	DIFFICULTY	A.I. GRADE
20 minutes	50 minutes	●●○○○	Good

DIRECTIONS

1. Put the rice in a pot and cover it with water and 1 tsp of salt.
2. Bring to a boil and continue cooking for another 45 minutes.
3. Meanwhile, take the avocado pulp and cut it into cubes.
4. Place the avocado in a bowl and add the crabmeat.
5. Season with salt, pepper and lemon juice and mix well.
6. When the rice is ready, drain it and leave it to cool.
7. Pour the rice into the bowl with the avocado, add the mint leaves and the oil and mix well.
8. Now divide the rice into two plates and serve.

NUTRITIONAL VALUES:

CARBS	PROTEINS	FATS	CALORIES
38gr	14gr	9gr	419

FIRST COURSE RECIPES

Black rice with chicken and vegetables

INGREDIENTS FOR 2 SERVINGS

- 5 oz of black rice
- 1 small zucchini
- 1 carrot
- 10.5 oz of chicken breast
- 2 tbsp of olive oil
- Salt and pepper to taste

INGREDIENTS FOR 3 SERVINGS

- 7.5 oz of black rice
- 1 big size zucchini
- 2 carrots
- 16 oz of chicken breast
- 3 tbsp of olive oil
- Salt and pepper to taste

PREP. TIME	COOKING TIME	DIFFICULTY	A.I. GRADE
25 minutes	50 minutes	●●○○○	Good

DIRECTIONS

1. Bring a pot of water and 1 tsp of salt to a boil. Add the rice and cook for 45 minutes.
2. Wash the zucchini and carrots, cut them into cubes and cook them in a saucepan with boiling water and salt for 10 minutes. After cooking, drain them and leave them to cool.
3. Brush the chicken breast with olive oil, sprinkle with salt and pepper and cook on a hot grill, for 10 minutes per side.
4. When the chicken is cooked, place it on a cutting board and cut it into cubes.
5. Drain the rice and put it in a bowl. Add the vegetables and chicken. Season with oil and pepper and mix well.
6. Divide the rice with the chicken and vegetables between two plates and serve.

NUTRITIONAL VALUES:

CARBS	PROTEINS	FATS	CALORIES
36gr	14gr	10gr	370

FIRST COURSE RECIPES

Black rice with salmon

INGREDIENTS FOR 2 SERVINGS

- 5 oz of black rice
- 3.5 oz of smoked salmon
- 1.7 oz of cherry tomatoes
- ½ clove of garlic
- 1 tbsp chopped parsley
- Salt and black pepper to taste
- Olive oil to taste

INGREDIENTS FOR 3 SERVINGS

- 7.5 oz of black rice
- 5.7 oz of smoked salmon
- 2.5 oz of cherry tomatoes
- 1 garlic clove
- 2 tbsp chopped parsley
- Salt and black pepper to taste
- Olive oil to taste

PREP. TIME	COOKING TIME	DIFFICULTY	A.I. GRADE
20 minutes	50 minutes	●●○○○	Good

DIRECTIONS

1. First, cook the rice in boiling salted water for 45 minutes and then drain it.
2. In the meantime, wash the cherry tomatoes and cut them into 4 parts.
3. Cut the salmon into thin slices.
4. Heat a little oil in a pan and sauté the garlic.
5. After a couple of minutes, add the cherry tomatoes and cook for 5 minutes.
6. Add the salmon, cook for another two minutes then switch off, season with pepper, and remove the garlic clove.
7. Pour the rice into the pan with the salmon and cherry tomatoes, mix well and then divide it into two plates.
8. Sprinkle with the parsley and then serve.

NUTRITIONAL VALUES:

CARBS	PROTEINS	FATS	CALORIES
29gr	19gr	12gr	318

FIRST COURSE RECIPES

Brown rice with chicken and mint

INGREDIENTS FOR 2 SERVINGS

- 5 oz of brown rice
- 8.8 oz of chicken breast
- 1 red pepper
- ½ onion
- 4 mint leaves
- 2 tbsp of olive oil
- Salt and pepper to taste

INGREDIENTS FOR 3 SERVINGS

- 7.5 oz of brown rice
- 13.4 oz of chicken breast
- 2 red peppers
- 1 onion
- 6 mint leaves
- 3 tbsp of olive oil
- Salt and pepper to taste

PREP. TIME	COOKING TIME	DIFFICULTY	A.I. GRADE
25 minutes	45 minutes	●●○○○	Good

DIRECTIONS

1. First, put water with 1 tsp of salt in a pot and bring it to a boil. Pour the rice and cook for 40 minutes.
2. Wash the pepper, cut it in half, remove the seeds and filaments and cut it into small pieces.
3. Chop the onion and sauté it in a pan with olive oil.
4. Then add the pepper, add salt, and pepper and cook for 15 minutes.
5. Brush the chicken with olive oil, season with salt and pepper and cook on a hot plate for 10 minutes on each side. After cooking, put it on a cutting board and cut it into cubes.
6. Once cooked, drain the rice, and pass it for a few seconds under cold water.
7. Put the rice in a bowl and add the peppers, chopped mint leaves and chicken.
8. Season with oil and pepper and mix well.
9. Now divide the rice with the chicken and the peppers between two plates and serve.

NUTRITIONAL VALUES:

CARBS	PROTEINS	FATS	CALORIES
32gr	18gr	6gr	378

Brown rice with zucchini, tuna, and avocado

INGREDIENTS FOR 2 SERVINGS

- 4.2 oz of brown rice
- 7 oz tuna in oil, drained
- 2 small zucchinis
- 1 clove of garlic
- 1 small avocado
- 2 basil leaves
- Olive oil to taste
- Salt and pepper to taste

INGREDIENTS FOR 3 SERVINGS

- 6.3 oz of brown rice
- 10.5 oz tuna in oil, drained
- 3 small zucchinis
- 2 garlic cloves
- 1 large size avocado
- 3 basil leaves
- Olive oil to taste
- Salt and pepper to taste

PREP. TIME	COOKING TIME	DIFFICULTY	A.I. GRADE
25 minutes	45 minutes	●●○○○	Good

DIRECTIONS

1. Put water in a saucepan with 1 tsp of salt, bring to a boil and then add the rice. Cook for 40 minutes.
2. Wash the zucchini and then cut them into cubes.
3. Transfer the zucchini to the pan with a tbsp of olive oil, the peeled garlic clove and some salt and pepper. Cover with lid and cook for 10 min.
4. When the rice is cooked, drain it, and let it cool.
5. Peel the avocado, remove the pulp, and cut it into cubes.
6. Put the rice in a bowl and add the drained tuna.
7. Cut the basil leaves into strips and place them in the bowl with the tuna.
8. Add the zucchini and avocado, season with oil and pepper and mix well.
9. Now divide the rice into two plates and serve.

NUTRITIONAL VALUES:

CARBS	PROTEINS	FATS	CALORIES
39gr	19gr	10gr	385

FIRST COURSE RECIPES

Buddha bowl with black rice and chicken

INGREDIENTS FOR 2 SERVINGS

- 5 oz of black rice
- ½ avocado
- 2 oz cherry tomatoes
- 8.4 oz of chicken breast
- 1 tbsp of olive oil
- 2 tbsp soy sauce
- Salt and black pepper to taste

INGREDIENTS FOR 3 SERVINGS

- 7.5 oz of black rice
- 1 avocado
- 3 oz cherry tomatoes
- 12.8 oz of chicken breast
- 2 tbsp of olive oil
- 3 tbsp soy sauce
- Salt and black pepper to taste

PREP. TIME	COOKING TIME	DIFFICULTY	A.I. GRADE
30 minutes	45 minutes	●●○○○	Good

DIRECTIONS

1. Put the rice in a pot covered with water. Add 1 tsp of salt and bring to a boil. From now on, cook for 40 minutes.
2. Meanwhile, cut the chicken breast into equal-sized cubes.
3. Heat the olive oil in a pan and then add the chicken cubes.
4. Cook for 6 minutes, then add salt and pepper, mix well, and switch off.
5. Now wash and cut the cherry tomatoes in half.
6. When the rice has finished cooking, drain it, and let it cool.
7. Then put the rice in the bottom of two bowls.
8. Peel the avocado, cut the pulp into cubes, and place it in a corner of the bowl.
9. Then add the chicken and finally the cherry tomatoes.
10. Sprinkle with soy sauce and serve.

NUTRITIONAL VALUES:

CARBS	PROTEINS	FATS	CALORIES
33gr	12gr	6gr	375

FIRST COURSE RECIPES

Carrot, spring onion and ginger cream

INGREDIENTS FOR 2 SERVINGS

- 3 large carrots
- 2 spring onions
- 2 cups of vegetable broth
- 1 tsp fresh grated ginger
- Salt and pepper to taste
- Olive oil to taste

INGREDIENTS FOR 3 SERVINGS

- 3 large carrots
- 2 spring onions
- 2 cups of vegetable broth
- 1 tsp fresh grated ginger
- Salt and pepper to taste
- Olive oil to taste

PREP. TIME	COOKING TIME	DIFFICULTY	A.I. GRADE
15 minutes	35 minutes	●●○○○	Top

DIRECTIONS

1. Wash the spring onions and cut them into small pieces.
2. Wash the carrots, peel them, and cut them into pieces.
3. Heat 1 tbsp of oil in a pan and then sauté the spring onions.
4. Wait 5 minutes and then add the carrots.
5. Season with salt and pepper, add the broth and cook for 20 minutes.
6. After 20 minutes, add the ginger, mix, and continue cooking for another 10 minutes.
7. After 10 minutes, switch off and blend everything with an immersion blender.
8. When you have obtained a thick and velvety cream, stop the blender, and divide the cream into two plates.
9. Season the cream of carrots, spring onions and ginger with a drizzle of oil and serve.

NUTRITIONAL VALUES:

CARBS	PROTEINS	FATS	CALORIES
14gr	4gr	3gr	92

FIRST COURSE RECIPES

Chilled Cucumber Ginger Soup

INGREDIENTS FOR 2 SERVINGS

- 2 cucumbers
- 2.2 oz of Greek yogurt
- 2 tbsp fresh grated ginger
- 2 lemongrass leaves
- 2 cherry tomatoes
- 1 tbsp extra virgin olive oil
- 1 tsp of garlic-flavored oil
- Salt and pepper to taste

INGREDIENTS FOR 3 SERVINGS

- 3 cucumbers
- 3.3 oz of Greek yogurt
- 3 tbsp fresh grated ginger
- 3 lemongrass leaves
- 3 cherry tomatoes
- 2 tbsp extra virgin olive oil
- 2 tsp of garlic flavored oil
- Salt and pepper to taste

PREP. TIME	COOKING TIME	DIFFICULTY	A.I. GRADE
20 minutes	/	●●○○○	Top

DIRECTIONS

1. Wash and peel the cucumbers, cut them in half lengthwise and remove the seeds with a teaspoon. Slice the cucumbers, salt them, and put them in a colander.
2. Put the cucumbers, yoghurt, ginger, and lemongrass leaves in the blender glass, activate the blender and when the soup becomes smooth, slowly add the garlic oil and the extra virgin olive oil and blend for another 30 seconds.
3. Divide the soup into two bowls.
4. Wash the cherry tomatoes, cut them into cubes and put them on top of the soup.
5. Drizzle with a drizzle of oil and serve.

NUTRITIONAL VALUES:

CARBS	PROTEINS	FATS	CALORIES
5gr	6gr	2gr	46

FIRST COURSE RECIPES

Cream of asparagus

**INGREDIENTS
FOR 2 SERVINGS**

- 7 oz of asparagus
- 1 carrot
- ½ onion
- 1.7 oz of low fat Greek yogurt
- 2 cups of vegetable broth
- 1 tbsp of olive oil
- 1 tsp of salt
- Black pepper to taste

**INGREDIENTS
FOR 3 SERVINGS**

- 10.5 oz of asparagus
- 2 carrots
- 1 onion
- 2.8 oz of low fat Greek yogurt
- 3 cups of vegetable broth
- 2 tbsp of olive oil
- 2 tsp of salt
- Black pepper to taste

PREP. TIME	COOKING TIME	DIFFICULTY	A.I. GRADE
15 minutes	25 minutes	●●○○○	Top

DIRECTIONS

1. Wash the asparagus, remove the hard part, and then cut them into slices.
2. Chop the onion and brown it in a pan with the hot olive oil.
3. Add the asparagus, the peeled and chopped carrot and the salt.
4. Stir, cook for 1 minute and then add the broth.
5. Cook for 20 minutes, then switch off and add the Greek yogurt.
6. Blend the soup with an immersion blender until you get a thick and velvety cream.
7. Divide the cream between two plates, season with a little black pepper and serve.

NUTRITIONAL VALUES:

CARBS	PROTEINS	FATS	CALORIES
12gr	4gr	2gr	143

FIRST COURSE RECIPES

Cream of beans and shrimp

INGREDIENTS FOR 2 SERVINGS

- 4 shrimp tails
- ½ clove of garlic
- 1 sprig of rosemary
- 1 tomato
- 7 oz of pre-soaked red kidney beans
- Salt and black pepper to taste
- Olive oil to taste

INGREDIENTS FOR 3 SERVINGS

- 6 shrimp tails
- 1 clove of garlic
- 2 sprigs of rosemary
- 1 big size tomato
- 10.5 oz of pre-soaked red kidney beans
- Salt and black pepper to taste
- Olive oil to taste

PREP. TIME	COOKING TIME	DIFFICULTY	A.I. GRADE
20 minutes	75 minutes	●●●○○	Top

DIRECTIONS

1. Peel the garlic.
2. Heat 1 tbsp of oil with the garlic clove and rosemary sprig, washed and dried, in a saucepan for 2 minutes over medium heat.
3. Now add the beans, cover them with cold water and season with salt and pepper.
4. Cook for 70 minutes, stirring occasionally.
5. Ten minutes before the beans are finished cooking, peel the shrimp tails, and wash them.
6. Heat a little oil in a pan and sauté the prawn tails for 3 minutes.
7. Wash the tomato and then cut it into cubes.
8. When the beans are cooked, remove the garlic and rosemary, and blend them with an immersion blender until you obtain a cream-like mixture.
9. Pour the cream of beans into two plates.
10. Sprinkle with the tomato cubes and then add the shrimp tails.
11. Season with oil and black pepper and serve.

NUTRITIONAL VALUES:

CARBS	PROTEINS	FATS	CALORIES
24gr	17gr	9gr	246

FIRST COURSE RECIPES

Cream of beans, salmon, and celery

INGREDIENTS FOR 2 SERVINGS

- 8.8 oz of cannellini beans
- 2 cups of vegetable broth
- ½ stalk of celery
- 3.5 oz of salmon fillet
- 2 sage leaves
- ½ clove of garlic
- Salt and pepper to taste
- Olive oil to taste

INGREDIENTS FOR 3 SERVINGS

- 13.2 oz of cannellini beans
- 3 cups of vegetable broth
- 1 stalk of celery
- 5.7 oz of salmon fillet
- 3 sage leaves
- 1 clove of garlic
- Salt and pepper to taste
- Olive oil to taste

PREP. TIME	COOKING TIME	DIFFICULTY	A.I. GRADE
20 minutes	95 minutes	●●○○○	Top

DIRECTIONS

1. Start by putting the beans the night before in a bowl covered with water.
2. The next day, peel the garlic and brown it in a pan with olive oil and sage leaves.
3. Add the beans, salt, and pepper, mix, and cook for a few seconds. Then add the broth.
4. Cook for 90 minutes, stirring occasionally.
5. While the beans are cooking, cut the salmon and celery into cubes.
6. Once the beans are cooked, remove the sage and garlic. Take an immersion blender and blend until you get a soft cream.
7. Put the cream of beans on two plates, add the salmon and celery, season with a drizzle of oil and serve.

NUTRITIONAL VALUES:

CARBS	PROTEINS	FATS	CALORIES
27gr	19gr	9gr	297

FIRST COURSE RECIPES

Cream of broad beans and peas

INGREDIENTS
FOR 2 SERVINGS

- 7 oz of broad beans
- 7 oz of peas
- ½ carrot
- 1 shallot
- 1.7 oz of Greek yogurt
- 2 cups of vegetable broth
- Olive oil to taste
- Salt to taste

INGREDIENTS
FOR 3 SERVINGS

- 10.5 oz of broad beans
- 10.5 oz of peas
- 1 carrot
- 1 shallot
- 2.8 oz of Greek yogurt
- 3 cups of vegetable broth
- Olive oil to taste
- Salt to taste

PREP. TIME	COOKING TIME	DIFFICULTY	A.I. GRADE
25 minutes	35 minutes	●●○○○	Top

DIRECTIONS

1. Shell the peas and broad beans by peeling the latter.
2. Peel the carrot and cut it into pieces.
3. Chop the shallot and brown it in a pan with a tbsp of olive oil.
4. At this point, add the peas, broad beans and carrot, salt and cook for 5 minutes.
5. Cover the legumes with hot broth and cook for 20 minutes.
6. If necessary, add more broth a little at a time until all the ingredients are cooked, but without leaving too much liquid in the pot.
7. After cooking, switch off and use an immersion blender and blend until you obtain a velvety and homogeneous cream.
8. Divide the cream between two plates, add the Greek yogurt and a drizzle of oil and serve.

NUTRITIONAL VALUES:

CARBS	PROTEINS	FATS	CALORIES
18gr	6gr	4gr	146

FIRST COURSE RECIPES

Cream of pumpkin and mushrooms

**INGREDIENTS
FOR 2 SERVINGS**

- 14 oz pumpkin
- 1 carrot
- 4.4 oz of mushrooms
- ½ shallot
- 2 cups of vegetable broth
- 1 clove of garlic
- 1 tbsp chopped coriander
- 4 tbsp Greek yogurt
- Salt and pepper to taste
- Olive oil to taste

**INGREDIENTS
FOR 3 SERVINGS**

- 21 oz pumpkin
- 2 carrots
- 6.6 oz of mushrooms
- 1 shallot
- 3 cups of vegetable broth
- 1 clove of garlic
- 2 tbsp chopped coriander
- 6 tbsp Greek yogurt
- Salt and pepper to taste
- Olive oil to taste

PREP. TIME	COOKING TIME	DIFFICULTY	A.I. GRADE
25 minutes	30 minutes	●●●○○	Top

DIRECTIONS

1. Peel the pumpkin, remove the seeds, and cut the pulp into small pieces.
2. Clean the mushrooms, removing the stem and all the parts covered with soil and then cut them into slices.
3. Chop the shallot and garlic and put them to brown in a pan with hot olive oil.
4. Then add the pumpkin and mushrooms, salt, and pepper, mix well and cook for 1 minute.
5. Cover with the broth and cook for 20 minutes.
6. After cooking, turn off the heat and add the Greek yogurt.
7. Blend everything with an immersion blender until you obtain a thick and homogeneous cream.
8. Divide the mushroom and pumpkin cream between two plates, dress it with a drizzle of oil and a little pepper and serve.

NUTRITIONAL VALUES:

CARBS	PROTEINS	FATS	CALORIES
9gr	3gr	6gr	144

FIRST COURSE RECIPES

Cream of pumpkin and shrimp

INGREDIENTS FOR 2 SERVINGS

- 8.8 oz pumpkin
- 7 oz of shrimp
- 1 tbsp of olive oil
- 1 sprig of rosemary
- ½ clove of garlic
- ½ tsp sweet paprika
- Salt and pepper to taste

INGREDIENTS FOR 3 SERVINGS

- 13.4 oz pumpkin
- 10.5 oz of shrimp
- 2 tbsp of olive oil
- 2 sprigs of rosemary
- 1 clove of garlic
- 1 tsp sweet paprika
- Salt and pepper to taste

PREP. TIME	COOKING TIME	DIFFICULTY	A.I. GRADE
20 minutes	25 minutes	●●●○○	Top

DIRECTIONS

1. Peel the pumpkin, remove the seeds, and cut the pulp into cubes.
2. Peel the garlic clove.
3. Put the garlic to brown for a couple of minutes in a pan with a drizzle of oil.
4. Add the rosemary, and pumpkin and add paprika, salt and pepper.
5. Cover the pumpkin with warm water and cook for 20 minutes.
6. Meanwhile, shell the shrimps, wash them and cook them in a pan for 3 minutes with a drizzle of hot olive oil. After 3 minutes, add salt and pepper, mix, and then switch off.
7. When the pumpkin is ready, turn off the heat and remove the garlic and rosemary.
8. Use an immersion blender and blend the pumpkin until you get a thick and velvety cream.
9. Divide the pumpkin cream between two plates, add the sautéed prawns and serve.

NUTRITIONAL VALUES:

CARBS	PROTEINS	FATS	CALORIES
14gr	8gr	7gr	156

FIRST COURSE RECIPES

Lentil and mushroom soup

INGREDIENTS FOR 2 SERVINGS

- 7 oz of lentils
- 3.5 oz of mushrooms
- ½ carrot
- ½ onion
- 1 stalk of celery
- 3 cups of vegetable broth
- Olive oil to taste
- Salt and pepper to taste

INGREDIENTS FOR 3 SERVINGS

- 10.5 oz of lentils
- 5.7 oz of mushrooms
- 1 carrot
- 1 onion
- 2 stalks of celery
- 5 cups of vegetable broth
- Olive oil to taste
- Salt and pepper to taste

PREP. TIME	COOKING TIME	DIFFICULTY	A.I. GRADE
20 minutes	1 hour and 35 min.	●●○○○	Top

DIRECTIONS

1. Peel the onion and carrot, then chop them together with the celery.
2. Clean the mushrooms well, remove all the soil and then cut them into small pieces.
3. Heat a little olive oil in a pan and then add the onion, celery, and carrot.
4. Cook for 5 minutes and then add the mushrooms and lentils.
5. Season with salt and pepper and then pour in the broth.
6. Put the lid on the pan and cook for 1 hour and 30 minutes.
7. Once cooked, divide the lentil and mushroom soup into two plates, drizzle with a drizzle of oil and serve.

NUTRITIONAL VALUES:

CARBS	PROTEINS	FATS	CALORIES
28gr	4gr	5gr	369

FIRST COURSE RECIPES

Mushroom and hazelnut soup

INGREDIENTS FOR 2 SERVINGS

- 1 tbsp of toasted hazelnut grains
- 1 tbsp chopped parsley
- 1 tbsp chopped leeks
- ½ clove of garlic
- 1 tbsp extra virgin olive oil
- 8.8 oz of mixed mushrooms
- 2 cups of vegetable broth
- 4 tbsp Greek yogurt
- Salt and pepper to taste

INGREDIENTS FOR 3 SERVINGS

- 2 tbsp of toasted hazelnut grains
- 2 tbsp chopped parsley
- 2 tbsp chopped leeks
- 1 clove of garlic
- 2 tbsp extra virgin olive oil
- 13.4 oz of mixed mushrooms
- 3 cups of vegetable broth
- 6 tbsp Greek yogurt
- Salt and pepper to taste

PREP. TIME	COOKING TIME	DIFFICULTY	A.I. GRADE
20 minutes	20 minutes	●●○○○	Top

DIRECTIONS

1. Remove the stems from the mushrooms and clean them carefully, removing all the earthy parts and then cutting them into slices.
2. Peel the garlic.
3. Put the oil to heat in a pan and then add the garlic and leeks and cook for 2 minutes.
4. Add the mushrooms, salt, and pepper, mix and cook for 1 minute.
5. Add the broth and continue cooking for another 15 minutes.
6. After cooking, turn off the heat and add the yoghurt.
7. Blend with an immersion blender until you obtain a thick and velvety cream.
8. Divide the soup into two plates, sprinkle with parsley and chopped hazelnuts and serve.

NUTRITIONAL VALUES:

CARBS	PROTEINS	FATS	CALORIES
12gr	8gr	8gr	208

FIRST COURSE RECIPES

Pasta salad with avocado and tuna

INGREDIENTS FOR 2 SERVINGS

- 5 oz of durum wheat pasta
- ½ large avocado
- 1 ripe red tomato
- 1.7 oz tuna in oil, drained
- 1 oz of red onion
- Olive oil to taste
- Salt and pepper to taste

INGREDIENTS FOR 3 SERVINGS

- 7.5 oz of durum wheat pasta
- 1 large avocado
- 1 ripe red tomato
- 3.5 oz tuna in oil, drained
- 1.5 oz of red onion
- Olive oil to taste
- Salt and pepper to taste

PREP. TIME	COOKING TIME	DIFFICULTY	A.I. GRADE
20 minutes	20 minutes	●●○○○	Good

DIRECTIONS

1. Boil water and a teaspoon of salt in a saucepan.
2. Put the pasta and cook for 10 minutes.
3. Once cooked, drain the pasta, and leave it to cool.
4. Meanwhile, wash the tomato and cut it into small pieces.
5. Peel the onion and cut it into slices.
6. Peel the avocado and cut the pulp into cubes.
7. Put the pasta in a bowl and add the avocado, tomato, tuna, and onion.
8. Add oil and pepper and mix everything well.
9. Now divide the pasta salad into two plates and serve.

NUTRITIONAL VALUES:

CARBS	PROTEINS	FATS	CALORIES
32gr	18gr	12gr	315

Pasta salad with green bean cream

FIRST COURSE RECIPES

INGREDIENTS FOR 2 SERVINGS

- 4.2 oz of whole-wheat pasta
- 7 oz of green beans
- 10 cherry tomatoes
- 3.5 oz of Greek yogurt
- 1 clove of garlic
- 2 basil leaves
- 2 tbsp of olive oil
- Salt and pepper to taste

INGREDIENTS FOR 3 SERVINGS

- 6.3 oz of whole-wheat pasta
- 10.5 oz of green beans
- 15 cherry tomatoes
- 5.7 oz of Greek yogurt
- 1 clove of garlic
- 3 basil leaves
- 3 tbsp of olive oil
- Salt and pepper to taste

PREP. TIME	COOKING TIME	DIFFICULTY	A.I. GRADE
20 minutes	40 minutes	●●○○○	Good

DIRECTIONS

1. Remove the two ends of the green beans and then wash them.
2. Bring water to a boil with a little salt and cook the green beans for 20 minutes.
3. Once cooked, drain, and blend them together with the yogurt, basil, minced garlic, salt and pepper until you obtain a soft and thick cream.
4. Put the water and salt in another pan and bring to a boil. Add the pasta and cook for 10 minutes.
5. Meanwhile, wash the cherry tomatoes and cut them into small pieces.
6. Once cooked, drain the pasta, pass it under cold water and put it in a bowl.
7. Add the cream of green beans, and the cherry tomatoes and drizzle with the olive oil.
8. Mix well, then divide the pasta into two plates and serve.

NUTRITIONAL VALUES:

CARBS	PROTEINS	FATS	CALORIES
12gr	8gr	8gr	208

FIRST COURSE RECIPES

Pepper and Carrot Soup

INGREDIENTS FOR 2 SERVINGS

- 8.8 oz of red peppers
- 1 carrot
- 1 tbsp chopped onion
- 1 tbsp chopped celery
- 1 tbsp extra virgin olive oil
- 1 cup of vegetable broth
- 5 tbsp of Greek yogurt

INGREDIENTS FOR 3 SERVINGS

- 13.4 oz of red peppers
- 1 carrot
- 2 tbsp chopped onion
- 2 tbsp chopped celery
- 2 tbsp extra virgin olive oil
- 1 cup and ½ of vegetable broth
- 8 tbsp of Greek yogurt

PREP. TIME	COOKING TIME	DIFFICULTY	A.I. GRADE
20 minutes	35 minutes	●●○○○	Top

DIRECTIONS

1. Peel the carrot and grate it finely.
2. Wash the peppers, remove the seeds, and then cut them into thin slices.
3. Take a saucepan and pour 1 tbsp of extra virgin olive oil, put it on a medium-low flame and add the chopped onion, celery, and carrots, making them dry well.
4. Add the peppers, salt, pepper, and broth and cook for 30 minutes.
5. After 30 minutes, switch off and add the Greek yogurt and blend everything with an immersion blender.
6. Divide the soup between two plates and serve.

NUTRITIONAL VALUES:

CARBS	PROTEINS	FATS	CALORIES
10gr	6gr	3gr	100

Poke bowl with shrimp

FIRST COURSE RECIPES

INGREDIENTS FOR 2 SERVINGS

- 4.9 oz of black rice
- 8.8 oz of shrimp
- 1 small avocado
- ½ head of lettuce
- 2 small carrots
- 10 black olives
- ½ lemon
- 2 tbsp soy sauce
- Olive oil to taste
- Salt and pepper to taste

INGREDIENTS FOR 3 SERVINGS

- 7.4 oz of black rice
- 13.4 oz of shrimp
- 1 avocado
- ½ head of lettuce
- 3 small carrots
- 15 black olives
- 1 lemon
- 3 tbsp soy sauce
- Olive oil to taste
- Salt and pepper to taste

PREP. TIME	COOKING TIME	DIFFICULTY	A.I. GRADE
20 minutes	45 minutes	●●○○○	Good

DIRECTIONS

1. Start by preparing the rice. Put the rice in a pot with water and salt, bring it to a boil and then let it cook for 40 minutes.
2. In the meantime, wash the lettuce, dry it, and then cut it into small pieces.
3. Peel the carrots and cut them into thin slices.
4. Remove the head and carapace from the shrimps, then remove the black filament with the aid of a toothpick and rinse them. Season with a drizzle of oil, a drop of lemon juice, and a pinch of salt and pepper and then cook them for 2 minutes on each side on a hot grill.
5. Open the avocado, peel it, and cut it into thin slices, then dress it with a little lemon juice.
6. Once cooked, drain the rice, and let it cool.
7. Now put the rice in the bottom of two bowls.
8. Put the lettuce, carrots, avocado and finally the prawns on top.
9. Drizzle with oil and soy sauce and serve.

NUTRITIONAL VALUES:

CARBS	PROTEINS	FATS	CALORIES
31gr	12gr	9gr	288

FIRST COURSE RECIPES

Rice with spinach and salmon

INGREDIENTS FOR 2 SERVINGS

- 4.9 oz of brown rice
- 2 cups of water
- 7 oz of spinach leaves
- 7 oz of smoked salmon
- 1 clove of garlic
- 1 tsp of chopped dill
- 1 tbsp of olive oil
- Salt and pepper to taste

INGREDIENTS FOR 3 SERVINGS

- 7.4 oz of brown rice
- 3 cups of water
- 10.5 oz of spinach leaves
- 10.5oz of smoked salmon
- 1 clove of garlic
- 2 tsp of chopped dill
- 2 tbsp of olive oil
- Salt and pepper to taste

PREP. TIME	COOKING TIME	DIFFICULTY	A.I. GRADE
20 minutes	55 minutes	●●○○○	Good

DIRECTIONS

1. Wash the spinach and put them in a pan with the oil and the garlic clove.
2. Add a glass of water and cook for 10 minutes, stirring occasionally.
3. After 10 minutes, add the rice and toast for 2 minutes.
4. Season with salt and pepper and cover the rice with water.
5. Stir and cover the pan with the lid.
6. Cook for 40 minutes, stirring often and adding more water if necessary.
7. After cooking, switch off and add the smoked salmon cut into thin slices.
8. Divide the rice between two plates, sprinkle with the chives and serve.

NUTRITIONAL VALUES:

CARBS	PROTEINS	FATS	CALORIES
32gr	22gr	12gr	338

FIRST COURSE RECIPES

Saffron leek cream

**INGREDIENTS
FOR 2 SERVINGS**

- 5 leeks
- ½ tsp of saffron powder
- 2 cups of vegetable broth
- Salt and pepper to taste
- 1 tbsp of olive oil

**INGREDIENTS
FOR 3 SERVINGS**

- 8 leeks
- ½ tsp of saffron powder
- 3 cups of vegetable broth
- Salt and pepper to taste
- 2 tbsp of olive oil

PREP. TIME	COOKING TIME	DIFFICULTY	A.I. GRADE
20 minutes	25 minutes	●●○○○	Good

DIRECTIONS

1. Remove the green part of the leeks and the outer leaves. Wash them and cut them into slices.
2. Heat the oil in a pan and then put the leeks to sauté for a couple of minutes.
3. Season with salt and pepper, add the broth and put the lid on the pan.
4. Cook for 15 minutes, stirring occasionally and then add the saffron.
5. Stir again and cook for another 2 minutes.
6. After 2 minutes, switch off and blend everything with an immersion blender.
7. Divide the cream of leeks between two plates, season with oil and pepper and serve.

NUTRITIONAL VALUES:

CARBS	PROTEINS	FATS	CALORIES
11gr	3gr	3gr	176

FIRST COURSE RECIPES

Spaghetti with shrimp and cherry tomatoes

INGREDIENTS FOR 2 SERVINGS

- 5 oz of whole-wheat spaghetti
- 5.2 oz of cherry tomatoes
- 6.3 oz of shrimp
- 1 clove of garlic
- 2 basil leaves
- Salt and pepper to taste
- Olive oil

INGREDIENTS FOR 3 SERVINGS

- 7.5 oz of whole-wheat spaghetti
- 7.8 oz of cherry tomatoes
- 9.4 oz of shrimp
- 1 clove of garlic
- 3 basil leaves
- Salt and pepper to taste
- Olive oil

PREP. TIME	COOKING TIME	DIFFICULTY	A.I. GRADE
20 minutes	15 minutes	●●○○○	Good

DIRECTIONS

1. First, clean the shrimps: pass them under running water, and remove the head, legs, carapace, and intestine.
2. Peel and cut the garlic into thin slices.
3. Pour a drizzle of oil into the pan and sauté the sliced garlic.
4. Wash the cherry tomatoes, cut them in half and put them in the pan with the garlic.
5. Cook for 5 minutes, and in the meantime, boil water and 1 tsp of salt in a saucepan.
6. When the water starts to boil, add the spaghetti, and cook for 10 minutes.
7. Now add the shrimp to the pan with the cherry tomatoes, season with salt and pepper and continue cooking for another 10 minutes.
8. Drain the spaghetti and put them in the pan with the cherry tomatoes and the shrimp.
9. Mix well and then divide the pasta and sauce between two plates.
10. Add the basil cut into strips and serve.

NUTRITIONAL VALUES:

CARBS	PROTEINS	FATS	CALORIES
34gr	16gr	7gr	375

FIRST COURSE RECIPES

Spaghetti with tuna and pumpkin

INGREDIENTS FOR 2 SERVINGS

- 5 oz of whole-wheat spaghetti
- 4.4 oz pumpkin pulp
- 1 tbsp chopped onion
- 3.5 oz of tuna in oil
- 1 tsp of olive oil
- Salt and black pepper to taste

INGREDIENTS FOR 3 SERVINGS

- 7.5 oz of whole-wheat spaghetti
- 6.6 oz pumpkin pulp
- 2 tbsp chopped onion
- 5.7 oz of tuna in oil
- 1 tbsp of olive oil
- Salt and black pepper to taste

PREP. TIME	COOKING TIME	DIFFICULTY	A.I. GRADE
20 minutes	20 minutes	●●○○○	Good

DIRECTIONS

1. Wash the pumpkin pulp and cut it into small cubes.
2. Heat the oil in a pan and put the onion to brown for a few minutes.
3. Add the pumpkin, season with salt and pepper and cook for 10 minutes.
4. After 10 minutes, drain the tuna and put it in the pan with the pumpkin.
5. Mix well, cook for 2 minutes, and then switch off.
6. Put water and a tsp of salt in a saucepan and bring to a boil.
7. Add the spaghetti and cook for 10 minutes.
8. Drain the pasta and then put it in the pan with the pumpkin and tuna.
9. Add a couple of tablespoons of pasta cooking water and turn the stove back on.
10. Mix well, cook for 1 minute and switch off.
11. Divide the pasta between two plates and serve.

NUTRITIONAL VALUES:

CARBS	PROTEINS	FATS	CALORIES
31gr	18gr	8gr	372

FIRST COURSE RECIPES

Spaghetti with zucchini

INGREDIENTS FOR 2 SERVINGS

- 5 oz of whole-wheat spaghetti
- 10.5 oz of zucchinis
- ½ clove of garlic
- 2 basil leaves
- Salt and pepper to taste
- Olive oil to taste

INGREDIENTS FOR 3 SERVINGS

- 7.5 oz of whole-wheat spaghetti
- 16 oz of zucchinis
- 1 clove of garlic
- 3 basil leaves
- Salt and pepper to taste
- Olive oil to taste

PREP. TIME	COOKING TIME	DIFFICULTY	A.I. GRADE
20 minutes	20 minutes	●●○○○	Good

DIRECTIONS

1. Wash the zucchinis and then grate them and set them aside.
2. Place water and 1 tsp of salt in a saucepan and bring to a boil.
3. Add the spaghetti and cook for 10 minutes.
4. Heat the oil in a pan together with the peeled garlic.
5. When the garlic has changed color, remove it and add the zucchini.
6. Season with salt and pepper and cook for 5 minutes, stirring frequently.
7. When the pasta is cooked, drain it, and pour 2 tbsp of the cooking water into the pan with the zucchini.
8. Then add the drained pasta, mix, and cook for 2 minutes.
9. After 2 minutes, divide the pasta into two plates and serve.

NUTRITIONAL VALUES:

CARBS	PROTEINS	FATS	CALORIES
53gr	10gr	5gr	349

FIRST COURSE RECIPES

Tomato lentil soup

INGREDIENTS FOR 2 SERVINGS

- 7 oz peeled tomatoes
- ½ carrot
- 1 shallot
- 2 oz of red lentils
- 1 cup of vegetable broth
- 4 fresh basil leaves
- Salt and pepper to taste
- 2 tbsp of olive oil

INGREDIENTS FOR 3 SERVINGS

- 10.5 oz peeled tomatoes
- 1 carrot
- 1 shallot
- 3 oz of red lentils
- 2 glasses of vegetable broth
- 6 fresh basil leaves
- Salt and pepper to taste
- 3 tbsp of olive oil

PREP. TIME	COOKING TIME	DIFFICULTY	A.I. GRADE
15 minutes	40 minutes	●●○○○	Good

DIRECTIONS

1. Peel the shallot and carrot and chop them.
2. Heat the oil in a pan and add the shallot and carrot. Brown briefly, add the tomato with all the liquid, add salt and pepper and cook for 15 minutes.
3. Rinse the lentils and put them in the pan. Add the vegetable broth and cook for another 20 minutes.
4. After 20 minutes, switch off and add the basil leaves cut into strips.
5. Now divide the soup into two plates, drizzle with a drizzle of oil and serve.

NUTRITIONAL VALUES:

CARBS	PROTEINS	FATS	CALORIES
27gr	10gr	6gr	333

FIRST COURSE RECIPES

Tomato porridge

INGREDIENTS FOR 2 SERVINGS

- 3.5 oz of rolled oats
- 1 glass of water
- 2 eggs
- 7 oz of tomato puree
- ½ clove of garlic
- 2 tbsp blanched almonds
- 1 tbsp chopped parsley
- Salt to taste
- Olive oil to taste

INGREDIENTS FOR 3 SERVINGS

- 5.7 oz of rolled oats
- 1 glass and ½ of water
- 3 eggs
- 10.5 oz of tomato puree
- 1 clove of garlic
- 3 tbsp blanched almonds
- 2 tbsp chopped parsley
- Salt to taste
- Olive oil to taste

PREP. TIME	COOKING TIME	DIFFICULTY	A.I. GRADE
20 minutes	35 minutes	●●○○○	Good

DIRECTIONS

1. Put the eggs in a saucepan covered with cold water and bring to a boil. From now on, cook for another 9 minutes.
2. Now immerse the eggs in cold water to let them cool, then peel them and cut them into wedges.
3. Peel the garlic and sauté it for a couple of minutes in a pan with hot olive oil.
4. Remove the garlic and add the tomato puree.
5. Bring to a boil and then add the salt, stir, and cook for another 5 minutes.
6. Now add the water and bring it to a boil again.
7. Now pour the oatmeal and cook for 10 minutes, over low heat and stirring often.
8. After 10 minutes, switch off and transfer the porridge into two bowls.
9. Sprinkle with the almonds and chopped parsley, add the eggs, drizzle with a drizzle of olive oil and serve.

NUTRITIONAL VALUES:

CARBS	PROTEINS	FATS	CALORIES
48gr	15gr	8gr	354

FIRST COURSE RECIPES

Tomato soup

INGREDIENTS FOR 2 SERVINGS

- 21 oz of tomatoes
- 1.7 oz of Greek yogurt
- ½ clove of garlic
- 2 basil leaves
- Salt and pepper to taste
- Olive oil to taste

INGREDIENTS FOR 3 SERVINGS

- 32.5 oz of tomatoes
- 2.5 oz of Greek yogurt
- 1 clove of garlic
- 3 basil leaves
- Salt and pepper to taste
- Olive oil to taste

PREP. TIME	COOKING TIME	DIFFICULTY	A.I. GRADE
20 minutes	55 minutes	●●○○○	Top

DIRECTIONS

1. Wash the tomatoes, peel them, and cut them in half.
2. Remove the pulp and seeds and cut the rest into cubes.
3. Heat a tbsp of oil in a saucepan and add the peeled garlic. Brown the garlic and then add the tomato pieces.
4. Add the basil leaves, salt and pepper and cook for 30 minutes.
5. After 30 minutes, lower the heat to a minimum, remove the garlic and blend the rest with an immersion blender.
6. Add the yogurt, mix well, and cook for another 20 minutes, stirring occasionally.
7. After 20 minutes, switch off and put the soup on two plates.
8. Season the soup with a drizzle of oil and serve.

NUTRITIONAL VALUES:

CARBS	PROTEINS	FATS	CALORIES
14gr	4gr	9gr	72

FIRST COURSE RECIPES

Whole-wheat pasta with peppers

INGREDIENTS FOR 2 SERVINGS

- 4.2 oz of whole-wheat penne
- 5.2 oz of red peppers
- ½ shallot
- Salt and pepper to taste
- Olive oil to taste

INGREDIENTS FOR 3 SERVINGS

- 6.6 oz of whole-wheat penne
- 7.8 oz of red peppers
- 1 shallot
- Salt and pepper to taste
- Olive oil to taste

PREP. TIME	COOKING TIME	DIFFICULTY	A.I. GRADE
20 minutes	20 minutes	●●○○○	Good

DIRECTIONS

1. Chop the shallot.
2. Wash the peppers, remove the seeds, and then cut them into cubes.
3. Put the peppers and shallots in a saucepan, add salt and pepper and cover the bottom with water. Put on the heat and cook for 15 minutes, stirring occasionally.
4. Boil a saucepan with water and 1 tsp of salt and then put the penne to cook for 8-10 minutes, according to the instructions on the package.
5. When the peppers are ready, blend them with an immersion blender until you obtain a thick and homogeneous cream.
6. Drain the pasta and pour it into the pan with the peppers.
7. Mix well, then divide the pasta into two plates and serve.

NUTRITIONAL VALUES:

CARBS	PROTEINS	FATS	CALORIES
24gr	4gr	4gr	380

Whole-wheat spaghetti with lemon

INGREDIENTS FOR 2 SERVINGS

- 4.9 oz of whole-wheat spaghetti
- 2 tbsp of olive oil
- ½ lemon
- 1 tbsp chopped parsley
- Salt and pepper to taste

INGREDIENTS FOR 3 SERVINGS

- 7.4 oz of whole-wheat spaghetti
- 3 tbsp of olive oil
- 1 lemon
- 2 tbsp chopped parsley
- Salt and pepper to taste

PREP. TIME	COOKING TIME	DIFFICULTY	A.I. GRADE
15 minutes	15 minutes	●●○○○	Good

DIRECTIONS

1. First, bring a pot of water and 1 tsp of salt to a boil.
2. Add the spaghetti and cook for 10 minutes.
3. Meanwhile, wash the lemon, grate the zest, and squeeze the juice into a bowl.
4. Put the olive oil in a pan and let it heat up.
5. Add the lemon juice and zest, salt and pepper and cook for 3 minutes, then switch off.
6. When the spaghetti is cooked, drain it, and put it in the pan with the sauce.
7. Mix well, then divide the spaghetti into two plates and serve.

NUTRITIONAL VALUES:

CARBS	PROTEINS	FATS	CALORIES
33gr	2gr	6gr	356

SECOND COURSE RECIPES

Almond and spice breaded cod

INGREDIENTS FOR 2 SERVINGS

- 1 already cod fillet sliced (4 slices)
- 2 tsp of olive oil
- 3 tbsp of almond flour
- ½ tsp of paprika
- 1 tbsp of fish mixed spices
- Salt and pepper to taste

INGREDIENTS FOR 3 SERVINGS

- 1 already cod fillet sliced (6 slices)
- 3 tsp of olive oil
- 5 tbsp of almond flour
- 1 tsp of paprika
- 2 tbsp of fish mixed spices
- Salt and pepper to taste

PREP. TIME	COOKING TIME	DIFFICULTY	A.I. GRADE
20 minutes	25 minutes	●●○○○	Good

DIRECTIONS

1. As the first thing to do, put the cod slices in a bowl and drizzle with oil, taking care that they're well coated.
2. So, in a shallow dish, mix the almond flour with the spices until well combined.
3. Coat each cod slice in almond spicy breading, and transfer to your baking pan.
4. At the same time, preheat your oven to 400°F.
5. Once the temperature is reached place breaded almond cod in the oven and let cook for 15/20 minutes about.
6. But, after the first 10 minutes have passed, open the oven, and flip the cod to the other side then keep on cooking.
7. Serve the breaded spicy cod slices still hot.

NUTRITIONAL VALUES:

CARBS	PROTEINS	FATS	CALORIES
8gr	32gr	3gr	340

SECOND COURSE RECIPES

Asparagus and vinegar tuna

INGREDIENTS FOR 2 SERVINGS

- 10.5 oz of tuna fillet
- 7 oz of green asparagus
- 4 tbsp of apple cider vinegar
- 1 tsp of turmeric powder
- Olive oil to taste
- Salt and pepper to taste

INGREDIENTS FOR 3 SERVINGS

- 16 oz of tuna fillet
- 10.5 oz of green asparagus
- 6 tbsp of apple cider vinegar
- 2 tsp of turmeric powder
- Olive oil to taste
- Salt and pepper to taste

PREP. TIME	COOKING TIME	DIFFICULTY	A.I. GRADE
20 minutes	20 minutes	●●○○○	Good

DIRECTIONS

1. Start by taking away the hardest part from the asparagus, so wash them and then let them drain.
2. Now, place a pot of water and salt to a boil and then put the asparagus to blanch for 5 minutes.
3. Once blanched, drain the asparagus, and set aside.
4. Wash and dry the tuna fillet.
5. So, brush a baking pan with olive oil and then put the tuna and boiled asparagus inside.
6. At the same time, in a small bowl put together vinegar, turmeric and 1 tsp of olive oil, salt and pepper.
7. Stir well until you get a homogeneous emulsion.
8. Sprinkle the fish with the turmeric and vinegar emulsion and then place the pan in the oven.
9. Arrange the baking pan on the oven rack and cook at 400 °F for 10 minutes.
10. Once cooked, take out the tuna fillet from the oven and let it rest for 5 minutes.
11. After 5 minutes, cut the tuna into some slices and place it, along with the asparagus, on serving plates.
12. Sprinkle with the vinegar and turmeric cooking juices and serve.

NUTRITIONAL VALUES:

CARBS	PROTEINS	FATS	CALORIES
5gr	36gr	14 gr	380

SECOND COURSE RECIPES

Avocado and grapefruit Alaska Pollock

INGREDIENTS FOR 2 SERVINGS

- 4 slices of Alaska Pollock of 3.5 oz each
- 1 avocado
- 2 sprigs of rosemary
- ½ onion
- 1 pink grapefruit
- 3.5 oz of almond flour
- Salt and pepper to taste
- Olive oil to taste

INGREDIENTS FOR 3 SERVINGS

- 6 slices of Alaska Pollock of 3.5 oz each
- 2 avocados
- 3 sprigs of rosemary
- 1 onion
- 1 pink grapefruit
- 5.7 oz of almond flour
- Salt and pepper to taste
- Olive oil to tastee

PREP. TIME	COOKING TIME	DIFFICULTY	A.I. GRADE
25 minutes	25 minutes	●●●○○	Good

DIRECTIONS

1. Wash and dry the already cleaned Alaska Pollock slices and dry.
2. Wash and dry the rosemary too and then chop the leaves.
3. Now, you can also wash and dry the pink grapefruit. Grate its zest and strain the fresh juice into a bowl.
4. Join the almond flour, rosemary, grapefruit zest, salt, and pepper in a bowl.
5. Combine well and then flour the Alaska Pollock slices.
6. Peel the half onion, wash it, and then mince it.
7. Peel, pit and cut the avocado into some cubes.
8. Heat two tablespoons of olive oil in a pan and, once hot, put the onion to dry.
9. Add the avocado cubes and cook them for 10 minutes.
10. Season with salt and pepper and then take out the ingredients of the pan and set aside.
11. Now put the fish slices and cook them for 3 minutes per side
12. Now add the avocado again, grapefruit juice and cook for another 5 minutes, so season with salt and pepper and turn off.
13. Put the Alaska Pollock slices and avocado on serving plates, sprinkle with the pink grapefruit cooking juices and serve.

NUTRITIONAL VALUES:

CARBS	PROTEINS	FATS	CALORIES
5gr	32gr	6gr	330

SECOND COURSE RECIPES

Basil pistachio and turmeric mackerel

INGREDIENTS FOR 2 SERVINGS

- 14 oz of already cleaned mackerel fillets
- 1 tbsp of olive oil
- 1 tbsp of chopped basil leaves
- 2 tsp of chopped pistachios
- 1 tsp of powdered turmeric
- 1 lime zest
- Salt and pepper to taste

INGREDIENTS FOR 3 SERVINGS

- 21.5 oz of already cleaned mackerel fillets
- 2 tbsp of olive oil
- 2 tbsp of chopped basil leaves
- 3 tsp of chopped pistachios
- 2 tsp of powdered turmeric
- 1 lime zest
- Salt and pepper to taste

PREP. TIME	COOKING TIME	DIFFICULTY	A.I. GRADE
15 minutes	15 minutes	●●●○○	Good

DIRECTIONS

1. Start this anti-inflammatory recipe by washing the already cleaned (boneless) mackerel fillet under running water, so rinse it and dry it with the help of a paper towel.
2. So, in a mortar, crush both basil and pistachios.
3. Done this, take the mackerel fillets and start flavoring them with salt and pepper. Add the mixed basil and pistachios and the powdered turmeric.
4. Place the mackerel fillets in a baking tray with a parchment paper put on top and sprinkle them with olive oil and the lime zest on top.
5. Bake in the oven at 375°F for 13/15 minutes.
6. When the mackerel fillets with turmeric and basil are well baked, serve them still hot.

NUTRITIONAL VALUES:

CARBS	PROTEINS	FATS	CALORIES
5gr	32gr	6gr	330

SECOND COURSE RECIPES

Broccoli jalapeño tilapia

INGREDIENTS FOR 2 SERVINGS

- 13 oz of tilapia fillets
- 12 broccoli tops
- 1 tsp of chopped jalapeno
- ½ tsp of ginger powder
- 1 tsp of chopped parsley
- ½ lime juice
- 2 tsp of olive oil
- Salt and pepper to taste

INGREDIENTS FOR 3 SERVINGS

- 19.5 oz of tilapia fillets
- 18 broccoli tops
- 1 tsp of chopped jalapeno
- 1 tsp of ginger powder
- 2 tsp of chopped parsley
- 1 lime juice
- 3 tsp of olive oil
- Salt and pepper to taste

PREP. TIME	COOKING TIME	DIFFICULTY	A.I. GRADE
15 minutes	25 minutes	●●○○○	Good

DIRECTIONS

1. As first step for this recipe, wash and dry all the broccoli tops, chopping them into many pieces. Wash and chop the parsley too.
2. Take any bones away from the tilapia fillet, then wash and dry it.
3. So, put together in a bowl, the olive oil, lime, salt, jalapeno and ginger powder, and pepper, with a fork. Stir until you get a spicy homogeneous emulsion.
4. So, grasp one sheet of aluminum foil and place the tilapia fillet inside. Add the minced broccoli, jalapeno and then wet everything with the lime and jalapeno emulsion.
5. Close the foil, being to seal it.
6. Put the tilapia and broccoli in the oven and cook at 340°F for 20/22 minutes.
7. Once ready, serve the jalapeno tilapia with the broccoli and sprinkle with the lime and ginger marinating anti-inflammatory liquid.

NUTRITIONAL VALUES:

CARBS	PROTEINS	FATS	CALORIES
5gr	38gr	4gr	360

SECOND COURSE RECIPES

Coconut milk and beets green salmon

INGREDIENTS FOR 2 SERVINGS

- 11 oz of salmon fillet
- 5.07 oz of beets green
- 2 tbsp of coconut milk
- 1 shallot
- 1 yolk
- 2 cups fish stock
- Salt and pepper to taste
- Olive oil to taste

INGREDIENTS FOR 3 SERVINGS

- 16.5 oz of salmon fillet
- 7 oz of beets green
- 3 tbsp of coconut milk
- 1 shallot
- 2 yolks
- 3 cups fish stock
- Salt and pepper to taste
- Olive oil to taste

PREP. TIME	COOKING TIME	DIFFICULTY	A.I. GRADE
35 minutes	20 minutes	●●○○○	Top

DIRECTIONS

1. As first step, wash and dry the salmon fillet. Take away any bone from it and then cut into cubes.
2. Wash and let the beets green to drain as well.
3. Now, peel and wash the shallot and then chop it.
4. So, you can heat 1 tbsp of olive oil in a pan.
5. Once hot, brown the just minced shallot.
6. When you will see that is golden brown, add the salmon cubes and brown for a couple of minutes.
7. Join the beets green to them, season with salt and pepper and mix well.
8. Keep on cooking just for 2 minutes and then add the fish stock.
9. Cook for another 10 minutes.
10. After 10 minutes has passed, add the yolk and coconut milk to the salmon.
11. Whip and cook for another 2 minutes.
12. Once all is well cooked, put the salmon with its coconut cream cooking juice on serving plates and serve.

NUTRITIONAL VALUES:

CARBS	PROTEINS	FATS	CALORIES
6gr	32gr	11gr	285

SECOND COURSE RECIPES

Ginger and jalapeno baked tuna

INGREDIENTS FOR 2 SERVINGS

- 1 tuna fillet of 14 oz about already cleaned
- 2 big sized limes
- 1 tsp of chopped chives
- 1 tsp of powdered ginger
- 1 tsp of chopped jalapeno
- olive oil to taste
- Salt to taste

INGREDIENTS FOR 3 SERVINGS

- 1 tuna fillet of 21 oz about already cleaned
- 3 big sized limes
- 2 tsp of chopped chives
- 2 tsp of powdered ginger
- 1 tsp of chopped jalapeno
- olive oil to taste
- Salt to taste

PREP. TIME	COOKING TIME	DIFFICULTY	A.I. GRADE
20 minutes	15 minutes	●●○○○	Top

DIRECTIONS

1. Start by washing and drying the tuna and place it in a baking tray brushed with some olive oil.
2. Wash and dry the two big sized limes, grate their zest, and squeeze the juice inside a pan. Join salt and olive oil to the lime juice and put together with a wooden spoon.
3. Now place the tuna fillet, sprinkle with coriander, ginger and jalapeno and cook in the hot oven at 400°F for 12 minutes.
4. When the tuna is well baked, halve, arrange it on serving plates and serve sprinkled with the lime and jalapeno cooking juices and the lime zest.

NUTRITIONAL VALUES:

CARBS	PROTEINS	FATS	CALORIES
1gr	28gr	10gr	290

SECOND COURSE RECIPES

Asparagus and honey salmon

INGREDIENTS FOR 2 SERVINGS

- 14 oz of salmon filet
- 7 oz of asparagus
- ¼ cup of honey
- 4 tbsp of apple cider vinegar
- Olive oil to taste
- Salt and pepper to taste

INGREDIENTS FOR 3 SERVINGS

- 21 oz of salmon filet
- 10.5 oz of asparagus
- 1/3 cup of honey
- 6 tbsp of apple cider vinegar
- Olive oil to taste
- Salt and pepper to taste

PREP. TIME	COOKING TIME	DIFFICULTY	A.I. GRADE
25 minutes	30 minutes	●●●○○	Top

DIRECTIONS

1. As first step for this recipe, take away the hardest part from the asparagus, wash them and then let them drain.
2. So, bring a pot of water and salt to a boil and then put the asparagus to blanch for 5 minutes.
3. Once cooked, drain the asparagus, and set aside.
4. Wash and dry the salmon fillet and take away excess of bones from it.
5. Heat 2 tablespoons of olive oil in a pan and, once hot, brown the fish, 3 minutes per side.
6. Season the salmon fillet with a pinch of salt and pepper and turn off.
7. Brush a baking pan with some olive oil and then put the salmon and asparagus inside.
8. In a small bowl combine the honey, vinegar, 3 tsp of olive oil, salt and pepper.
9. Put together well until you get a homogeneous emulsion.
10. Sprinkle the salmon fillet with the emulsion and then arrange the pan in the oven.
11. Cook at 400 °F for 10 minutes.
12. Once cooked, take the salmon out of the oven, and let it rest for 5 minutes.
13. After 5 minutes of rest, cut the fish into slices and place it, together with the asparagus, on serving plates.
14. Sprinkle with the cooking juices and serve this salmon dish.

NUTRITIONAL VALUES:

CARBS	PROTEINS	FATS	CALORIES
10gr	32gr	11gr	390

SECOND COURSE RECIPES

Kale and berries plaice

INGREDIENTS FOR 2 SERVINGS

- 9 oz of plaice fillet
- ½ cup of kale
- Half a shallot
- ¼ cup of red berries
- 1 bay leaf
- 1 tbsp of olive oil
- 2 tbsp of fish stock
- Salt and pepper to taste

INGREDIENTS FOR 3 SERVINGS

- 13.5 oz of plaice fillet
- 1 cup of kale
- 1 shallot
- 1/3 cup of red berries
- 1 bay leaf
- 2 tbsp of olive oil
- 3 tbsp of fish stock
- Salt and pepper to taste.

PREP. TIME	COOKING TIME	DIFFICULTY	A.I. GRADE
10 minutes	35 minutes	●●●○○	Good

DIRECTIONS

1. Start the anti-inflammatory recipe with the fish. Remove the excess of bones then wash and dry it.
2. Place the rack on a sheet of aluminum foil, brush the plaice fillet with a little of olive oil and then close the aluminum foil.
3. Arrange the foiled fish on a baking sheet.
4. Bake in the oven at 400°F for 20 minutes about.
5. Meanwhile, prepare the kale leaves.
6. Peel, wash and then finely mince the shallot.
7. Wash the kale, dry it, and then cut it into thin slices.
8. Wash and dry the bay leaves as well.
9. In a pan, put a drizzle of oil to heat. Once oil is hot, sauté the shallot for a couple of minutes, stirring constantly.
10. Now add the kale, flavor with salt and pepper and mix.
11. After 2 minutes, add the bay leaf, washed red fruits and fish broth.
12. Cook for 30 minutes, adding water if necessary, and stirring occasionally.
13. As soon as the plaice fillet is cooked, take it out of the oven, let the fish rest for 5 minutes and then slice it.
14. Put the kale and red fruits on the bottom of the serving dish, then over the plaice slices and sprinkle everything with the cooking juices of the kale and red fruits.

NUTRITIONAL VALUES:

CARBS	PROTEINS	FATS	CALORIES
3gr	34gr	2gr	290

SECOND COURSE RECIPES

Lettuce and tofu cheese salmon salad

INGREDIENTS FOR 2 SERVINGS

- 7 oz of smoked salmon
- ¼ cup of tofu cheese
- ½ cup of lettuce
- Olive oil to taste
- Salt and pepper to taste

INGREDIENTS FOR 3 SERVINGS

- 10.5 oz of smoked salmon
- 1 cup of tofu cheese
- 1 cup of lettuce
- Olive oil to taste
- Salt and pepper to taste

PREP. TIME	COOKING TIME	DIFFICULTY	A.I. GRADE
15 minutes	/	●○○○○	Top

DIRECTIONS

1. As first operation for this recipe, take the smoked salmon and cut it into thin slices.
2. Season the smoked salmon with olive oil, salt, and pepper.
3. So, now you can wash and dry the lettuce and then split into small pieces.
4. Arrange the lettuce in a bowl and flavor with oil, salt and pepper.
5. Now distribute the lettuce into two serving plates.
6. Place the strips of smoked salmon and tofu cheese on top.
7. Pour over a drizzle of oil and serve.

NUTRITIONAL VALUES:

CARBS	PROTEINS	FATS	CALORIES
3gr	34gr	9gr	280

SECOND COURSE RECIPES

Mushroom cream plaice fillet

INGREDIENTS FOR 2 SERVINGS

- 10.5 oz of button mushrooms
- 1 tsp of chopped red onion
- 10.5 oz of plaice fillet
- 2 tbsp of soy flour
- 2 cups of vegetable broth
- 2 tsp of chopped coriander
- 1 cup of sugar free vegetable milk
- Olive oil to taste
- Salt and pepper to taste

INGREDIENTS FOR 3 SERVINGS

- 16 oz of button mushrooms
- 2 tsp of chopped red onion
- 16 oz of plaice fillet
- 3 tbsp of soy flour
- 3 cups of vegetable broth
- 3 tsp of chopped coriander
- 1 cup and ½ of sugar free vegetable milk
- Olive oil to taste
- Salt and pepper to taste

PREP. TIME	COOKING TIME	DIFFICULTY	A.I. GRADE
15 minutes	25 minutes	●●○○○	Good

DIRECTIONS

1. First, take away any earthy part of button mushrooms, so rinse very fast under running water, dry them and then slice them.
2. Clean the plaice fillet, eliminating any bone and rinse under running water too.
3. So, put a little of olive oil in a pan and, once it is hot enough, put the tsp of onion to brown.
4. Add the sliced mushrooms, and plaice fillet, season with salt and pepper and cook for 7/8 minutes. Now add the soy flour and the 2 cups of broth. Stir and keep on cooking for another 7 minutes.
5. Now add the vegetable milk and cook for another 4 minutes. After cooking has done, turn off and remove the fish. Take all the rest of ingredients with an immersion blender, blend until you will have a very creamy mixture.
6. Put the button mushroom cream into serving dishes.
7. Place the fish fillet on top, drizzle with a drizzle of oil and chopped coriander and serve.

NUTRITIONAL VALUES:

CARBS	PROTEINS	FATS	CALORIES
4gr	29gr	5gr	310

SECOND COURSE RECIPES

Orange and avocado halibut

INGREDIENTS FOR 2 SERVINGS

- 2 halibut steaks (7 oz for each)
- 3 tsp of olive oil
- 1 blood orange
- ½ avocado
- ½ scallion
- 1 tsp of chives
- ½ tsp of powdered ginger
- Salt and pepper to taste
- A sprig of chopped cilantro

INGREDIENTS FOR 3 SERVINGS

- 3 halibut steaks (7 oz for each)
- 5 tsp of olive oil
- 1 blood orange
- 1 avocado
- 1 scallion
- 2 tsp of chives
- 1 tsp of powdered ginger
- Salt and pepper to taste
- A sprig of chopped cilantro

PREP. TIME	COOKING TIME	DIFFICULTY	A.I. GRADE
15 minutes	20 minutes	●●○○○	Top

DIRECTIONS

1. As first thing to do, peel the avocado, remove the stone, and after have pitted it, wash and dry it. So, split it into cubes.
2. Peel and wash the scallion, so dry it and chop it.
3. Wash and dry the halibut steaks, removing the bone and then cut it into small pieces.
4. Wash and dry the blood orange, grate the peel, and set it aside and then squeeze the pulp and strain the juice into a bowl.
5. Put the halibut, salt, pepper, chives, olive oil, ginger, and scallion in the bowl with the blood orange juice.
6. Stir gently to combine everything.
7. Let sauté the halibut with the blood orange and ginger sauce for few minutes in a pan.
8. When it will be well cooked, serve the halibut in the center of the plate.
9. Add the avocado cubes, sprinkle with chopped cilantro, and serve this anti-inflammatory dish.

NUTRITIONAL VALUES:

CARBS	PROTEINS	FATS	CALORIES
2gr	32gr	18gr	380

SECOND COURSE RECIPES

Pecans and carrot creamy tuna

INGREDIENTS FOR 2 SERVINGS

- 2 cups of tuna fillets
- 3 sage leaves
- 1 small size carrot
- 1 tsp of powdered ginger
- 2 tbsp of chopped pecans
- 2 juniper berries
- 1/3 cup of apple cider vinegar
- Olive oil to taste
- Salt to taste

INGREDIENTS FOR 3 SERVINGS

- 3 cups of tuna fillets
- 4 sage leaves
- 1 small size carrot
- 1 tsp of powdered ginger
- 3 tbsp of chopped pecans
- 3 juniper berries
- ½ cup of apple cider vinegar
- Olive oil to taste
- Salt to taste

PREP. TIME	COOKING TIME	DIFFICULTY	A.I. GRADE
25 minutes	25 minutes	●●○○○	Good

DIRECTIONS

1. As first step for this tuna recipe, wash and dry the fish fillet.
2. Brush the tuna fillet with olive oil and sprinkle it with salt on both sides to flavor.
3. At this point, arrange the tuna fillet in a baking pan.
4. Peel, at the same time, and wash the small size carrot and then chop it.
5. Wash and dry bay leaves as well.
6. Put the carrot, chopped sage, powdered ginger and juniper berries in the roasting pan.
7. Sprinkle the ingredients with 1/3 cup of apple cider vinegar.
8. So, preheat your oven to the temperature of 400°F.
9. Put the baking pan in the oven and let cook the tune fillet for 20 minutes about.
10. Just cooked, take tuna out of the oven, and let it rest for 10 minutes.
11. Slice the tuna and place its slices on serving plates.
12. Put the cooking juices in the glass of the mixer together with 2 tsp of olive oil and the chopped pecans.
13. Activate the mixer and whisk until you get a smooth cream.
14. Sprinkle the baked tuna with the pecans sauce and serve.

NUTRITIONAL VALUES:

CARBS	PROTEINS	FATS	CALORIES
10gr	33gr	5gr	370

Pineapple turmeric and star anise sea bream

INGREDIENTS FOR 2 SERVINGS

- 14 oz of sea bream fillet slices
- Almond flour to taste
- ½ cup of fresh sugar free pineapple juice
- 1 tbsp of coconut milk
- 2 tsp of olive oil
- 1 star anise berry
- 1 tsp of chopped rosemary
- Salt to taste.
- Pepper as needed

INGREDIENTS FOR 3 SERVINGS

- 21 oz of sea bream fillet slices
- Almond flour to taste
- 1 cup of fresh sugar free pineapple juice
- 2 tbsp of coconut milk
- 3 tsp of olive oil
- 1 star anise berry
- 2 tsp of chopped rosemary
- Salt to taste.
- Pepper as needed.

PREP. TIME	COOKING TIME	DIFFICULTY	A.I. GRADE
15 minutes	20 minutes	●●○○○	Good

DIRECTIONS

1. First, take the already cleaned sea bream slices, wash and dry them.
2. Wash and dry the pineapple and take ½ cup of fresh juice.
3. Pass the fish slices in the almond flour, trying to cover all over their surface.
4. Grasp a pan and heat the olive oil. Once hot, brown the fish for 3 minutes on each side, or until they are golden brown on both sides.
5. Now add the pineapple juice. Let it evaporate, then flavor with salt and pepper.
6. Now add the coconut milk and star anise.
7. Keep on cooking for a couple of minutes over medium heat.
8. Once the cooking juices are a little absorbed, add the chopped rosemary to the sea bream, turn it a couple of times until it has absorbed the sauce well and take away from the heat.
9. Serve the coconut and pineapple sea bream piping hot and sprinkled with the cooking juices.

NUTRITIONAL VALUES:

CARBS	PROTEINS	FATS	CALORIES
9gr	30gr	6gr	320

SECOND COURSE RECIPES

Soy cheese and veggies cod

INGREDIENTS FOR 2 SERVINGS

- 14 oz of cod fillets
- 2 tbsp olive oil
- 3 tbsp of soy cheese
- 1 tsp of turmeric powder
- 2 garlic cloves minced
- salt and pepper to taste
- 2 chopped tomatoes
- 1 cup of chopped green cabbage
- 1 cup of spinach

INGREDIENTS FOR 3 SERVINGS

- 21 oz of cod fillets
- 3 tbsp olive oil
- 5 tbsp of soy cheese
- 2 tsp of turmeric powder
- 3 garlic cloves minced
- salt and pepper to taste
- 3 chopped tomatoes
- 1 cup and ½ of chopped green cabbage
- 1 cup and ½ of spinach

PREP. TIME	COOKING TIME	DIFFICULTY	A.I. GRADE
15 minutes	15 minutes	●●○○○	Good

DIRECTIONS

1. Start this recipe by washing and dry the cleaned (you should take away any bone from the fish) cod, then cut it into slices.
2. Meanwhile, wash green cabbage leaves and chop.
3. Wash spinach leaves as well.
4. So, also wash the 2 tomatoes and chop them.
5. Peel and mince the 2 garlic cloves.
6. Heat a little of olive oil in a large saucepan.
7. Add the sliced cod fillet, season with turmeric powder, salt and pepper.
8. Sauté for 3 minutes or until cod is golden and cooked through.
9. Add the minced garlic and sauté for another minute.
10. Add the diced tomato, chopped green cabbage, spinach, and soy cheese.
11. Cook for another 3-4 minutes or until the cabbage is cooked through.
12. Serve this anti-inflammatory dish still hot.

NUTRITIONAL VALUES:

CARBS	PROTEINS	FATS	CALORIES
9gr	36gr	14gr	380

SECOND COURSE RECIPES

Spinach herbs and nuts pangasius

INGREDIENTS FOR 2 SERVINGS

- 2 pangasius fillets of 7 oz for each
- 7 oz of fresh baby spinach
- ½ chopped scallion
- 1 orange
- 1 tsp of chopped chives
- 1 sprig of thyme
- 1 tsp of chopped coriander
- 2 tbsp of mixed nuts
- olive oil to taste
- Salt and pepper to taste

INGREDIENTS FOR 3 SERVINGS

- 3 pangasius fillets of 7 oz for each
- 10.5 oz of fresh baby spinach
- 1 chopped scallion
- 1 orange
- 2 tsp of chopped chives
- 2 sprigs of thyme
- 1 tsp of chopped coriander
- 3 tbsp of mixed nuts
- olive oil to taste
- Salt and pepper to taste

PREP. TIME	COOKING TIME	DIFFICULTY	A.I. GRADE
10 minutes	15 minutes	●●○○○	Top

DIRECTIONS

1. As first step for this recipe, clean the fresh baby spinach by washing them. Drain and chop the spinach leaves together with all the aromatic herbs you have chosen.
2. So, proceed by washing and drying the orange, grating its zest, and straining the juice into a bowl. At this point, join a little orange zest to the chopped herbs and spinach bowl.
3. Put together and mix, so then a tablespoon of olive oil, salt and pepper and the chopped scallion and nuts and combine again.
4. Now, you can brush a pan, lay the cleaned pangasius fillets inside and then cover their surface with the chopped herbs, spinach, and nuts. Bake in the oven at the temperature of 400 °F for 10/12 minutes.
5. Once the pangasius will be well cooked, take it out of the oven, arrange on serving plates, decorate with the rest of the grated orange zest and serve this anti-inflammatory dish.

NUTRITIONAL VALUES:

CARBS	PROTEINS	FATS	CALORIES
3gr	36gr	7gr	360

SECOND COURSE RECIPES

Steamed sage and ginger halibut

INGREDIENTS FOR 2 SERVINGS

- 2 halibut fillets of 7.5 oz about for each
- 2 tbsp of minced lime peel
- 1 tsp of chopped thyme
- 1 tsp of chopped sage
- 1 tsp of minced fresh ginger
- Olive oil to taste
- Salt and pepper to taste

INGREDIENTS FOR 3 SERVINGS

- 3 halibut fillets of 7.5 oz about for each
- 3 tbsp of minced lime peel
- 1 tsp of chopped thyme
- 1 tsp of chopped sage
- 2 tsp of minced fresh ginger
- Olive oil to taste
- Salt and pepper to taste

PREP. TIME	COOKING TIME	DIFFICULTY	A.I. GRADE
15 minutes	25 minutes	●●○○○	Good

DIRECTIONS

1. First, take away the bone from the halibut fillet, then wash it under running water and dry it with a paper towel.
2. So, grasp the base of the steamer and fill it with some water. Put both the chopped herbs (thyme and sage), lime zest, mince ginger and pepper inside. Once the water comes to a boil, put the halibut fillet in the steamer basket and sprinkle it with some salt.
3. Cook the halibut fillet, with the lid on, for 15/20 minutes about. After cooking time has passed, take the halibut out of the basket, and arrange it on a cutting board.
4. Slice the halibut, put it on serving plates and serve sprinkled with a bit of lime zest drizzle of raw olive oil.

NUTRITIONAL VALUES:

CARBS	PROTEINS	FATS	CALORIES
2gr	32gr	5gr	310

SECOND COURSE RECIPES

Tangerine and pineapple cod

INGREDIENTS FOR 2 SERVINGS

- 2 cod fillets of 7 oz each
- 2 tangerines
- 2 tbsp of mustard
- 1 cup of fresh sugar free pineapple juice
- Olive oil to taste
- Salt and pepper to taste

INGREDIENTS FOR 3 SERVINGS

- 3 cod fillets of 7 oz each
- 3 tangerines
- 3 tbsp of mustard
- 1 cup and 3 tbsp of fresh sugar free pineapple juice
- Olive oil to taste
- Salt and pepper to taste

PREP. TIME	COOKING TIME	DIFFICULTY	A.I. GRADE
20 minutes	20 minutes	●●●○○	Top

DIRECTIONS

1. As first thing to do, remove the bones, wash, and dry the cod fillets and then flavor with salt and pepper.
2. Wash and dry the 2 tangerines, so grate their zest and strain their juice into a bowl, adding the pineapple one.
3. Add the 2 tbsp mustard to and put together until you get a homogeneous mixture.
4. So, line a baking pan with olive oil and put the cod fillets inside.
5. Sprinkle them with the tangerine and pineapple emulsion and arrange the baking pan inside the oven.
6. Cook at 350 °F for 8 minutes, then turn them, and keep on cooking for another 8 minutes.
7. Once the cod fillet is ready, take it away from the oven and let it rest for 5/6 minutes.
8. Now put the cod on the serving plates.
9. Sprinkle the cod fillets with the tangerine and pineapple cooking juices, sprinkle them with the grated rind of the tangerines and serve.

NUTRITIONAL VALUES:

CARBS	PROTEINS	FATS	CALORIES
15gr	16gr	3gr	290

SECOND COURSE RECIPES

Tilapia with lime and pecans

INGREDIENTS FOR 2 SERVINGS

- 2 tilapia fillets of 7 oz about for each
- The juice of a lime
- 1 minced garlic clove
- 2 tsp of chopped pecans
- Olive oil to taste
- Salt and pepper to taste

INGREDIENTS FOR 3 SERVINGS

- 3 tilapia fillets of 7 oz about for each
- The juice of a lime
- 1 minced garlic clove
- 3 tsp of chopped pecans
- Olive oil to taste
- Salt and pepper to taste

PREP. TIME	COOKING TIME	DIFFICULTY	A.I. GRADE
20 minutes	10 minutes	●●○○○	Good

DIRECTIONS

1. For this easy made recipe, first, wash and dry the tilapia fillets, remove all bones and skin.
2. Peel and mince the garlic clove.
3. Marinate tilapia fillets for about 15 minutes in a bowl and join to them olive oil, salt and pepper, lime juice, minced garlic, and the 2 tsp of chopped pecans.
4. So, place a grill to heat. Once the marinating time has elapsed, drain the tilapia fillets from the marinade and set the liquid aside.
5. At the same time, the grill will be hot, and you can cook the tilapia fillets for a couple of minutes on both sides.
6. When they are grilled enough you can put the lime tilapia fillets on a serving dish sprinkled with the marinating sauce.

NUTRITIONAL VALUES:

CARBS	PROTEINS	FATS	CALORIES
8gr	32gr	9gr	370

SECOND COURSE RECIPES

Trout and zucchini fish meatballs

INGREDIENTS FOR 2 SERVINGS

- 5 oz of ground cooked trout fillet
- 3.5 of shredded zucchini
- 1 little egg
- 2 tsp of grated Soy cheese
- 1 garlic clove
- 2 mint leaves
- 2 tbsp of almond flour
- Olive oil to taste
- Salt and pepper to taste

INGREDIENTS FOR 3 SERVINGS

- 7.5 oz of ground cooked trout fillet
- 5.7 of shredded zucchini
- 2 eggs
- 3 tsp of grated Soy cheese
- 1 garlic clove
- 3 mint leaves
- 3 tbsp of almond flour
- Olive oil to taste
- Salt and pepper to taste

PREP. TIME	COOKING TIME	DIFFICULTY	A.I. GRADE
30 minutes	25 minutes	●●●○○	Top

DIRECTIONS

1. Start by peeling the garlic clove and chopping it.
2. Heat 1 tsp of olive oil in a pan and, once hot enough, put the garlic to brown.
3. Add the shredded zucchinis and ½ glass of water and cook for 10 minutes about.
4. Add salt and pepper and let them cool.
5. Now, grasp an immersion blender and blend the zucchini.
6. Put the garlic zucchini in a bowl and add the minced cooked trout fillet.
7. Join the chopped mint leaves in the bowl with the other ingredients.
8. So, put together the trout the egg, grated soy cheese, salt and pepper and start kneading with a fork.
9. Now add the almond flour, mix well and then start forming the fish and mint fish balls.
10. Wet your hands and make a total of 10 fish balls.
11. Heat now a tbsp of olive oil in a non-stick pan.
12. Once hot, place the trout and mint fish balls and sauté 2 minutes on each side.
13. So, cover the pan with a lid and keep on cooking for another 8/9 minutes.
14. Once cooked, turn off, arrange the trout fish balls on serving plates and serve immediately.

NUTRITIONAL VALUES:

CARBS	PROTEINS	FATS	CALORIES
6gr	35gr	10gr	380

SECOND COURSE RECIPES

Yogurt and mushrooms tuna fillet

INGREDIENTS FOR 2 SERVINGS

- 7 oz of tuna fillet
- 2 tbsp of low-fat white yogurt
- 6 button mushrooms
- 1 lemon
- Salt and pepper to taste
- Olive oil to taste

INGREDIENTS FOR 3 SERVINGS

- 10.5 oz of tuna fillet
- 3 tbsp of low-fat white yogurt
- 9 button mushrooms
- 1 lemon
- Salt and pepper to taste
- Olive oil to taste

PREP. TIME	COOKING TIME	DIFFICULTY	A.I. GRADE
15 minutes + 1 hours to rest in the fridge	/	●●○○○	Good

DIRECTIONS

1. As first thing to do, take away the earthy part from the button mushrooms. So, clean them and chop coarsely.
2. Put the chopped button mushrooms in a bowl. Add the low-fat yogurt, the filtered lemon juice, olive oil, salt, and pepper.
3. Whisk until you get a thick mixture.
4. Put the tuna fillet in 2 serving plates and flavor with oil, salt, and pepper.
5. Sprinkle the tuna slices with the low-fat yogurt sauce and then transfer the dishes to rest in the fridge for at least 55/60 minutes.
6. After this time, remove the tuna and mushroom tuna fillet from the fridge and serve.

NUTRITIONAL VALUES:

CARBS	PROTEINS	FATS	CALORIES
1gr	22gr	10gr	170

SECOND COURSE RECIPES

Zucchini and avocado turmeric salmon

INGREDIENTS FOR 2 SERVINGS

- 2 salmon fillets of 7 oz about for each
- 2 zucchinis
- 1 ripe avocado
- 1 orange juice
- 1 tsp of chopped rosemary
- 1 tsp of turmeric powder
- Olive oil to taste
- Salt and pepper to taste

INGREDIENTS FOR 3 SERVINGS

- 3 salmon fillets of 7 oz about for each
- 3 zucchinis
- 1 ripe avocado
- 1 orange juice
- 2 tsp of chopped rosemary
- 2 tsp of turmeric powder
- Olive oil to taste
- Salt and pepper to taste

PREP. TIME	COOKING TIME	DIFFICULTY	A.I. GRADE
20 minutes	15 minutes	●●○○○	Top

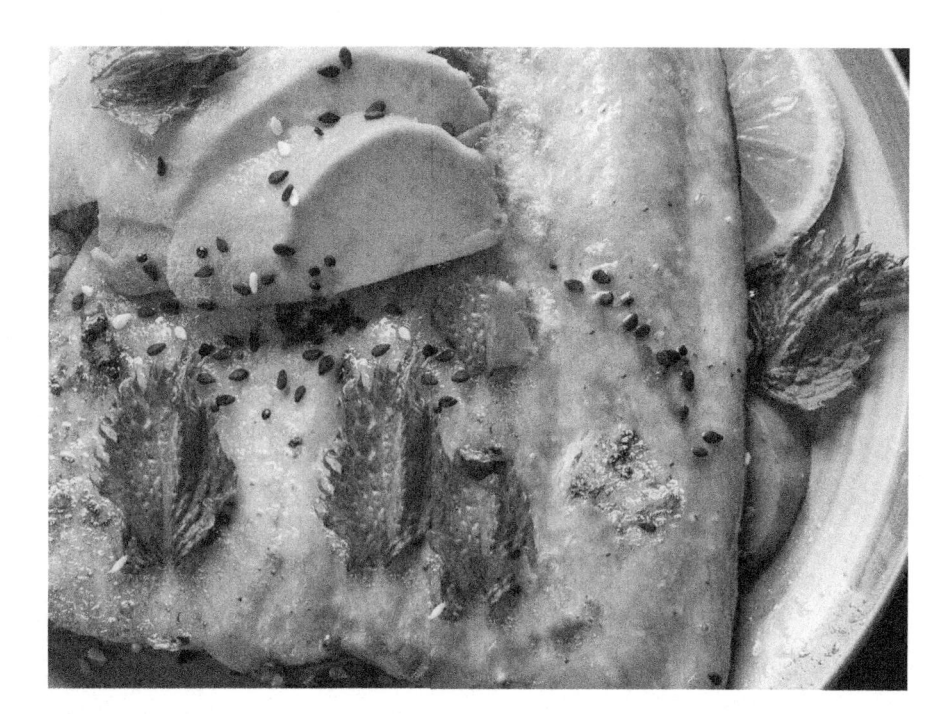

DIRECTIONS

1. As first operation for this salmon recipe, eliminate the bones from the salmon fillets, if still present, then rinse them under running water and let dry.
2. So, transfer the salmon fillets on a cutting board and, with the help of a knife, incise all the salmon skin.
3. Trim the 2 zucchinis, peel them, wash them, halve in a vertically manner and cut into cubes. Do the same (but remember to pit it) with the avocado.
4. Now, put the orange zest, zucchini, and avocado cubes, and chopped rosemary in the bowl with the orange juice too, put together and mix well. Now add the powdered turmeric and mix again. Season with salt and pepper
5. So, line a pan with a little of olive oil and place the zucchini and avocado cubes in the bottom of the pan. So, place the incised salmon fillets on top. Season the salmon with a little olive oil and a pinch of salt and pepper and then cook in the oven at 400°F for 13/15 minutes (but if you prefer you can cook the salmon less).
6. Once the cooking is ended, take the salmon away from the oven, place the zucchini and avocado cubes on the bottom of the plate and the salmon on top. You can serve this delicious salmon and veggies dish.

NUTRITIONAL VALUES:

CARBS	PROTEINS	FATS	CALORIES
2gr	32gr	16gr	390

SECOND COURSE RECIPES

Cauliflower chia seeds and ginger chicken

INGREDIENTS FOR 2 SERVINGS

- 14 oz of chicken breasts
- 10 cauliflower tops
- 1 tsp of fresh minced ginger
- ½ tsp of smoked paprika
- 1 tsp of chopped dill
- 1 tsp of chia seeds
- ½ lemon juice
- 2 tsp of olive oil
- Salt to taste

INGREDIENTS FOR 3 SERVINGS

- 21 oz of chicken breasts
- 15 cauliflower tops
- 2 tsp of fresh minced ginger
- 1 tsp of smoked paprika
- 1 tsp of chopped dill
- 1 tsp of chia seeds
- 1 lemon juice
- 3 tsp of olive oil
- Salt to taste

PREP. TIME	COOKING TIME	DIFFICULTY	A.I. GRADE
15 minutes	25 minutes	●●○○○	Good

DIRECTIONS

1. As first step for this recipe, wash and dry all the cauliflower tops, chopping them into many pieces. Wash and chop the dill too.
2. Take any excess of fat away from the chicken breast, then wash and dry it.
3. So, put together in a bowl, the olive oil, lemon, salt, paprika and fresh minced ginger, with a fork. Stir until you get a spicy homogeneous emulsion.
4. So, grasp one sheet of aluminum foil and place the chicken breast inside. Add the minced cauliflower and then wet everything with the lemon and ginger emulsion.
5. Close the foil, being to seal it.
6. Put the chicken and cauliflower in the oven and cook at 420°F for 20/22 minutes.
7. Once ready, serve the chicken with the cauliflower and sprinkled with the emulsion and 1 tsp of chia seeds.

NUTRITIONAL VALUES:

CARBS	PROTEINS	FATS	CALORIES
5gr	48gr	4gr	390

SECOND COURSE RECIPES

Chicken and veggies taste salad

INGREDIENTS FOR 2 SERVINGS

- 10 oz of sliced chicken roast
- 1 little size avocado
- 1 cucumber
- 2 tsp soy sauce
- 2 tsp of ginger powder
- 1 tsp turmeric powder
- 1 tbsp rice vinegar
- 2 tsp olive oil
- Chia seeds

INGREDIENTS FOR 3 SERVINGS

- 15 oz of sliced chicken roast
- 1 avocado
- 1 cucumber
- 3 tsp soy sauce
- 3 tsp of ginger powder
- 1 tsp turmeric powder
- 2 tbsp rice vinegar
- 3 tsp olive oil
- Chia seeds

PREP. TIME	COOKING TIME	DIFFICULTY	A.I. GRADE
15 minutes + 10 minutes to rest in the fridge	/	●●○○○	Top

DIRECTIONS

1. Start by preparing the anti-inflammatory salad marinade.
2. In a small bowl, pour the 2 tsp olive oil, rice vinegar soy sauce, ginger, and turmeric powder.
3. Now take the chicken roast and cut it into strips and put them in a bowl.
4. Pour the turmeric and ginger marinade over the chicken strips.
5. Cover the chicken and marinade with cling film and place in the fridge to flavor for 10 minutes.
6. So, move on to the veggies: divide the avocado in half lengthwise, remove the outer skin and the central stone and then cut it into cubes.
7. Wash the cucumber as well, halve and with a mandolin, or a peeler if you don't have a mandolin, cut the cucumber into thin strips.
8. Now take a bowl and put the chicken strips.
9. Join the cucumber and diced avocado.
10. So, complete decorating the salad with chia seeds, sprinkle everything with a little olive oil and a sprinkle of salt and pepper and serve this delicious salad.

NUTRITIONAL VALUES:

CARBS	PROTEINS	FATS	CALORIES
4gr	28gr	15gr	320

SECOND COURSE RECIPES

Cucumber turkey and grapefruit salad

INGREDIENTS FOR 2 SERVINGS

- 10.5 oz of roasted turkey slices
- ½ pink grapefruit
- 2 lettuce leaves
- ½ lemon
- ½ cucumber
- Olive oil to taste
- Salt and pepper to taste

INGREDIENTS FOR 3 SERVINGS

- 16 oz of roasted turkey slices
- 1 pink grapefruit
- 2 lettuce leaves
- 1 lemon
- 1 cucumber
- Olive oil to taste
- Salt and pepper to taste

PREP. TIME	COOKING TIME	DIFFICULTY	A.I. GRADE
10 minutes	/	●○○○○	Good

DIRECTIONS

1. As first step for this recipe, wash the grapefruit, peel it, and split it into wedges.
2. Peel the cucumber, remove the seeds, and then split it into slices (or cubes).
3. Put the cucumber and grapefruit in a bowl.
4. Add the sliced roasted turkey. Flavor with oil, salt, pepper, and the filtered lemon juice.
5. Gently mix all the anti-inflammatory salad ingredients and serve.

NUTRITIONAL VALUES:

CARBS	PROTEINS	FATS	CALORIES
7gr	30gr	3gr	270

SECOND COURSE RECIPES

Herbs and melon sauce chicken cubes

INGREDIENTS FOR 2 SERVINGS

- 14 oz of cubed chicken breast
- ¼ of a melon
- 2 mint leaves
- The zest of a lemon
- A sprig of parsley
- Salt and pepper to taste
- Olive oil to taste

INGREDIENTS FOR 3 SERVINGS

- 21.5 oz of cubed chicken breast
- ½ melon
- 3 mint leaves
- The zest of a lemon
- A sprig of parsley
- Salt and pepper to taste
- Olive oil to taste

PREP. TIME	COOKING TIME	DIFFICULTY	A.I. GRADE
15 minutes	15 minutes	●●○○○	GOOD

DIRECTIONS

1. First, grasp already washed chicken cubes and arrange them in the basket of the steamer, or in a colander and sprinkle them with a little salt.
2. Wash the mint, lemon peel and parsley.
3. Grind the base of the steamer, or alternatively a saucepan and put 2 cups of water inside. Put the aromatic herbs, the lemon peel, and a little pepper inside and bring to the boil.
4. Now put the basket with the chicken cubes and cook them for 12/15 minutes about.
5. In the meantime, peel the ¼ of melon, wash the pulp and then cut it.
6. Put the pulp in the mixer glass, add a little oil, salt and pepper and blend it.
7. Put the melon sauce on the bottom of the plates, spread over the steamed chicken cubes and serve.

NUTRITIONAL VALUES:

CARBS	PROTEINS	FATS	CALORIES
12gr	48gr	7gr	410

Anti Inflammatory

SECOND COURSE RECIPES

Garlic and pistachio turkey legs

INGREDIENTS FOR 2 SERVINGS

- 14 oz turkey legs
- 1 cup of apple cider vinegar
- 2 tbsp of chopped pistachios
- 2 garlic cloves
- Olive oil to taste
- Salt and pepper to taste

INGREDIENTS FOR 3 SERVINGS

- 21 oz turkey legs
- 1 cup and ½ of apple cider vinegar
- 3 tbsp of chopped pistachios
- 3 garlic cloves
- Olive oil to taste
- Salt and pepper to taste

PREP. TIME	COOKING TIME	DIFFICULTY	A.I. GRADE
25 minutes	70 minutes	●●●○○	Good

DIRECTIONS

1. As first step for this recipe, take away the excess fat from the turkey legs, then wash and pat the legs dry with a paper towel.
2. So, peel and wash the two garlic cloves and chop them.
3. Heat at this point, two tablespoons of olive oil in a pan.
4. Once hot enough, brown the turkey legs for 3 minutes on each side.
5. Turn off and then arrange the turkey legs in a baking pan brushed with olive oil.
6. Sprinkle the turkey legs with salt, pepper, minced garlic, and 2 tbsp of chopped pistachios.
7. Drizzle with apple cider vinegar and then place the baking pan in the oven.
8. Cook at 400 °F for 60 minutes, turning the turkey legs every 15 minutes and sprinkling it with their pistachio and garlic cooking juices.
9. Once cooked, take the turkey legs out of the oven, and let them rest for 5 minutes.
10. Put the legs on a cutting board and then divide into thin slices.
11. Put the turkey legs slices on serving plates, sprinkle with the garlic and pistachio cooking juices and serve.

NUTRITIONAL VALUES:

CARBS	PROTEINS	FATS	CALORIES
4gr	32gr	11gr	350

SECOND COURSE RECIPES

Mango and pineapple and chicken skewers

INGREDIENTS FOR 2 SERVINGS

- 14 oz of cubed chicken breast
- 2 limes
- 2 thyme sprigs
- 1 cup of cubed pineapple pulp
- 1 cup of cubed mango
- 1 scallion
- Salt and pepper to taste
- Olive oil to taste

INGREDIENTS FOR 3 SERVINGS

- 21 oz of cubed chicken breast
- 3 limes
- 3 thyme sprigs
- 1 cup and ½ of cubed pineapple pulp
- 1 cup and ½ of cubed mango
- 1 scallion
- Salt and pepper to taste
- Olive oil to taste

PREP. TIME	COOKING TIME	DIFFICULTY	A.I. GRADE
25 minutes + 40 minutes to rest in the fridge	20 minutes	●●●○○	GOOD

DIRECTIONS

1. As first operation for this skewer recipe, peel and wash the scallion and then chop it.
2. Wash and dry the thyme sprigs as well.
3. Wash and dry the chicken breast cubes.
4. Arrange now, the chicken meat in a bowl.
5. Join the thyme to the chicken, then add oil too, salt, pepper, minced scallions, and sprinkle with the filtered juice of the 2 limes.
6. Place a cling film over the bowl and put it to marinate in the fridge for at least 40 minutes.
7. After the marinating minutes, take the chicken back, drain it from the marinating liquid and start forming these delicious skewers.
8. Put the chicken cubes on the aluminum skewers.
9. Add pineapple and mango cubes and alternate ingredients until they will be done.
10. Heat a grill and, once hot, put the skewers to grill.
11. Cook for 3/4 minutes on each side and then remove from the grill.
12. Put the chicken and fruit skewers on serving plates, sprinkle with a little lemon marinating liquid and serve.

NUTRITIONAL VALUES:

CARBS	PROTEINS	FATS	CALORIES
18gr	32gr	3gr	370

SECOND COURSE RECIPES

Mustard and seeds chicken thighs

INGREDIENTS FOR 2 SERVINGS

- 2 chicken thighs of 7 oz each
- 3 tsp of mustard
- 1 tsp of mustard seeds
- 1 tsp of fennel seeds
- 1 scallion
- 1 tsp of chopped coriander
- Salt and pepper to taste
- Olive oil to taste

INGREDIENTS FOR 3 SERVINGS

- 3 chicken thighs of 7 oz each
- 5 tsp of mustard
- 2 tsp of mustard seeds
- 2 tsp of fennel seeds
- 1 scallion
- 2 tsp of chopped coriander
- Salt and pepper to taste
- Olive oil to taste

PREP. TIME	COOKING TIME	DIFFICULTY	A.I. GRADE
25 minutes	50 minutes	●●●○○	Good

DIRECTIONS

1. First, take away the skin from the chicken thighs and then wash and dry them.
2. Brush the thighs with some olive oil. Flavor them with salt and pepper and then brush them with mustard and sprinkle with mustard and fennel seeds.
3. So, line a baking pan with olive oil and then put the chicken thighs inside.
4. Peel and wash the scallion and then split it into slices.
5. Wash and dry the coriander and chop it.
6. Put the coriander in the baking pan with the chicken and then sprinkle with the scallion slices.
7. Arrange the baking pan in the oven and bake at 340 °F for 50 minutes.
8. Every 10 minutes, turn the chicken thighs and grind the liquid released by the meat a couple of times and wet the surface again.
9. Once cooked, take out the baking pan of the oven and let the chicken thighs rest for 5 minutes.
10. After 5 minutes, put the chicken thighs on serving plates.
11. Sprinkle with the mustard and seeds cooking juices and serve.

NUTRITIONAL VALUES:

CARBS	PROTEINS	FATS	CALORIES
7gr	34gr	10gr	340

SECOND COURSE RECIPES

Orange turkey and veggies

INGREDIENTS FOR 2 SERVINGS

- 2 turkey fillets of 5.7 oz for each
- 1 little size avocado
- 4 cherry tomatoes
- 1 lemon
- ½ cup of orange juice
- 1 tbsp of mixed herbs
- 1 tsp of smoked paprika
- 2 tsp of olive oil
- Salt and pepper to taste

INGREDIENTS FOR 3 SERVINGS

- 3 turkey fillets of 5.7 oz for each
- 1 large size avocado
- 6 cherry tomatoes
- 1 lemon
- 1 cup of orange juice
- 2 tbsp of mixed herbs
- 2 tsp of smoked paprika
- 3 tsp of olive oil
- Salt and pepper to taste

PREP. TIME	COOKING TIME	DIFFICULTY	A.I. GRADE
25 minutes	20 minutes	●●●○○	GOOD

DIRECTIONS

1. Let's start this anti-inflammatory recipe by cleaning the turkey. So, take away any excess of fat, wash it under running water, and let dry the meat.
2. Sprinkle the turkey breasts with a little salt and pepper and set aside.
3. Now move on to the avocado. Peel it, remove the stone, wash it under running water and then dry it. Now cut the avocado into thin strip.
4. Wash the cherry tomatoes too, dry them and then halve.
5. In a small bowl, now put together the orange juice, lemon juice, olive oil and the tbsp of chopped mixed herbs a pinch of salt and pepper. Stir well to mix everything.
6. So, take a pan large enough.
7. Put the turkey in the pan and brush it with a little olive oil.
8. Place the avocado on the bottom. Sprinkle them with a pinch of salt.
9. Now place the turkey breast on top of the avocado slices.
10. Place the cherry tomatoes on top of the turkey breast and then sprinkle everything with the orange marinade.
11. Arrange the pan to bake in a preheated oven at 400 °F for 15 minutes.
12. Check the cooking and, if necessary, continue cooking the turkey and veggies for another 5 minutes.
13. Serve the orange turkey with the avocado and cherry tomatoes.

NUTRITIONAL VALUES:

CARBS	PROTEINS	FATS	CALORIES
7gr	50gr	18gr	480

SECOND COURSE RECIPES

Radicchio and apple chicken salad

INGREDIENTS FOR 2 SERVINGS

- 7 oz of chicken breast
- 1 ripe apple
- ½ cup of radicchio leaves
- 1 sprig of thyme
- 2 sage leaves
- Apple cider vinegar to taste
- Olive oil to taste
- Salt and pepper to taste

INGREDIENTS FOR 3 SERVINGS

- 3 chicken thighs of 7 oz each
- 5 tsp of mustard
- 2 tsp of mustard seeds
- 2 tsp of fennel seeds
- 1 scallion
- 2 tsp of chopped coriander
- Salt and pepper to taste
- Olive oil to taste

PREP. TIME	COOKING TIME	DIFFICULTY	A.I. GRADE
25 minutes	50 minutes	●●●○○	Good

DIRECTIONS

1. First, take away the skin from the chicken thighs and then wash and dry them.
2. Brush the thighs with some olive oil. Flavor them with salt and pepper and then brush them with mustard and sprinkle with mustard and fennel seeds.
3. So, line a baking pan with olive oil and then put the chicken thighs inside.
4. Peel and wash the scallion and then split it into slices.
5. Wash and dry the coriander and chop it.
6. Put the coriander in the baking pan with the chicken and then sprinkle with the scallion slices.
7. Arrange the baking pan in the oven and bake at 340 °F for 50 minutes.
8. Every 10 minutes, turn the chicken thighs and grind the liquid released by the meat a couple of times and wet the surface again.
9. Once cooked, take out the baking pan of the oven and let the chicken thighs rest for 5 minutes.
10. After 5 minutes, put the chicken thighs on serving plates.
11. Sprinkle with the mustard and seeds cooking juices and serve.

NUTRITIONAL VALUES:

CARBS	PROTEINS	FATS	CALORIES
7gr	34gr	10gr	340

SECOND COURSE RECIPES

Sweet and sour turkey with asparagus

INGREDIENTS FOR 2 SERVINGS

- 14 oz of turkey breast
- 1 cup of fresh asparagus
- A lemon
- 3 tbsp of apple cider vinegar
- Green pepper and pink peppercorns to taste
- Salt and pepper to taste
- Olive oil to taste
- Chia seeds

INGREDIENTS FOR 3 SERVINGS

- 21.5 oz of turkey breast
- 1 cup and ½ of fresh asparagus
- A lemon
- 5 tbsp of apple cider vinegar
- Green pepper and pink peppercorns to taste
- Salt and pepper to taste
- Olive oil to taste
- Chia seeds

PREP. TIME	COOKING TIME	DIFFICULTY	A.I. GRADE
20 minutes	25 minutes	●●●○○	GOOD

+ 30 minutes to rest at room temperature

DIRECTIONS

1. First, take a fairly large bowl and put the vinegar, a spoonful of olive oil, salt and pepper and the filtered lemon juice inside.
2. Stir with a fork and mix well.
3. Wash and dry the turkey breast, take away from it the excess fat and cut it into cubes.
4. Place the turkey in the bowl with the marinade and marinate for 30 minutes at room temperature.
5. Trim the asparagus, wash and dry.
6. Boil a pot with water and salt then blanch the asparagus for 10 minutes.
7. After 10 minutes, drain the asparagus and let them cool.
8. Take a pan and heat some oil. Once hot, add the turkey with all the lemon marinade liquid.
9. Cook for 10 minutes and then add the asparagus. Stir, season with salt, add the pink and green pepper and cook for another 5 minutes.
10. Once the cooking time has elapsed, place the turkey on serving plates with the cooking liquid, sprinkle with the chia seeds and serve.

NUTRITIONAL VALUES:

CARBS	PROTEINS	FATS	CALORIES
2gr	48gr	7gr	390

SECOND COURSE RECIPES

Yogurt and chives chicken burger

INGREDIENTS FOR 2 SERVINGS

For the chicken burger:
- 7 oz ground chicken breast
- 1 tsp soy grated cheese
- ½ red onion.
- 1 tsp of fresh dill

For the yogurt sauce:
- 4 tbsp of low fat yogurt
- 1 tsp of mustard
- 1 tsp of fresh dill
- 1 tsp of chives

INGREDIENTS FOR 3 SERVINGS

For the chicken burger:
- 10.5 oz ground chicken breast
- 2 tsp soy grated cheese
- 1 red onion.
- 2 tsp of fresh dill

For the yogurt sauce:
- 6 tbsp of low fat yogurt
- 2 tsp of mustard
- 1 tsp of fresh dill
- 1 tsp of chives

PREP. TIME	COOKING TIME	DIFFICULTY	A.I. GRADE
25 minutes	15/20 minutes	●●●●○	Good

DIRECTIONS

1. Start by washing and chopping both dill and chives.
2. Meanwhile prepare the yogurt sauce putting together low-fat yogurt, dill, mustard and chives in a little dish.
3. Stir and set aside.
4. Peel wash and chop red onion as well.
5. So now, mix the ground chicken, soy, onion, and fresh dill.
6. When you will obtain a thick dough, forms 2 burgers.
7. Take a pan and heat with tiny quantities of olive oil. Cook chicken and dill burgers until browned for 7/8 minutes each side.
8. Serve, once cooked, these delicious chicken burgers with yogurt dill sauce.

NUTRITIONAL VALUES:

CARBS	PROTEINS	FATS	CALORIES
7gr	50gr	6gr	390

SECOND COURSE RECIPES

Zucchini and mushrooms chicken

INGREDIENTS FOR 2 SERVINGS

- 2 chicken breasts (7 oz for each)
- 2 Zucchinis
- 5 oz of mushrooms
- 1 garlic clove
- ½ orange
- 1 tsp of chopped chives
- Salt and pepper to taste

INGREDIENTS FOR 3 SERVINGS

- 3 chicken breast (7 oz for each)
- 3 Zucchini
- 7.5 oz of mushrooms
- 1 garlic clove
- 1 orange
- 1 tsp of chopped chives
- Salt and pepper to taste

PREP. TIME	COOKING TIME	DIFFICULTY	A.I. GRADE
20 minutes	35 minutes	●●●○○	GOOD

DIRECTIONS

1. As first step for this recipe, preheat your oven to 400 °F.
2. So, proceed the recipe by cleaning the chicken breast under running water, and drying it.
3. Keep, in the meantime, on washing the zucchini.
4. Clean the mushrooms too with the help of a cloth, taking away any soil.
5. Now, you can split the zucchini into slices and the mushrooms into 4 pieces.
6. So, peel and chop the garlic clove as well.
7. Pour over a baking paper on a baking sheet.
8. Arrange the veggies in the center of the pan.
9. Place the chicken breast on the side.
10. Flavor chicken now with salt and pepper.
11. Don't forget to squeeze the orange over the meat.
12. Add, at this point, the washed and chopped chives.
13. Close the parchment paper and make a sort of foil.
14. Cook the chicken in a preheated oven for about 30/35 minutes.
15. Always check the cooking of the chicken, zucchini, and mushrooms.
16. You can serve the chicken breast and veggies when they are perfectly cooked.

NUTRITIONAL VALUES:

CARBS	PROTEINS	FATS	CALORIES
3gr	49gr	4gr	390

SIDE DISHES RECIPES

Avocado and turkey omelette

INGREDIENTS FOR 2 SERVINGS

- 4 small size eggs
- 1 small size ripe avocado
- 1 tbsp of olive oil
- ¼ cup of sliced turkey roast
- 1 pinch of turmeric powder
- Salt and pepper to taste

INGREDIENTS FOR 3 SERVINGS

- 6 small size eggs
- 1 large size ripe avocado
- 2 tbsp of olive oil
- 1/3 cup of sliced turkey roast
- 1 tsp of turmeric powder
- Salt and pepper to taste

PREP. TIME	COOKING TIME	DIFFICULTY	A.I. GRADE
10 minutes	10 minutes	●●○○○	Good

DIRECTIONS

1. Start this anti-inflammatory recipe with avocado: peel and pit it, wash it, dry it and split into cubes.
2. Meanwhile pour the eggs in a bowl and batter them with a fork. Join to the eggs a pinch of salt, pepper, and turmeric powder, then mix the ingredients well. So, join the avocado and turkey roasted too.
3. Take a non-stick pan and heat a little bit oil and then add a little of battered egg, cooking them for 4/5 minutes on each side.
4. Close the avocado and turkey omelette, cook for another minute on each side and arrange it on a serving dish. You can serve this omelette.

NUTRITIONAL VALUES:

CARBS	PROTEINS	FATS	CALORIES
3gr	19gr	14gr	190

SIDE DISHES RECIPES

Baked ginger zucchini eggs and soy cheese

INGREDIENTS FOR 2 SERVINGS

- 1 cup of zucchinis
- 2 eggs
- 2 tsp of olive oil
- 1 tsp of fresh minced ginger
- 2 tbsp of soy cheese
- 1 tsp of chopped parsley
- Salt and pepper to taste

INGREDIENTS FOR 3 SERVINGS

- 1 cup and ½ of zucchinis
- 3 eggs
- 3 tsp of olive oil
- 3 tsp of fresh minced ginger
- 3 tbsp of soy cheese
- 1 tbsp of chopped parsley
- Salt and pepper to taste

PREP. TIME	COOKING TIME	DIFFICULTY	A.I. GRADE
25 minutes	35 minutes	●●●○○	GOOD

DIRECTIONS

1. First step for this recipe: cook the eggs in boiling water for 10 minutes maximum.
2. Once they are cooked, peel them, and cut them into small pieces. In the meantime, wash the zucchinis.
3. Then cut them into rounds, being careful not to cut them too thinly.
4. Brush one of the two tablespoons of oil in a bowl, distributing it over the entire surface.
5. Then lay the zucchini on top, trying not to overlap each other.
6. Now preheat the oven to 400°F.
7. Mix the chopped ginger in a dish together with the eggs and the soy cheese.
8. Add a pinch of salt, the pepper, and the chopped parsley.
9. Stir again to mix your dough.
10. Spread the soy cheese and ginger mixture thus obtained on the zucchinis, trying to distribute it evenly.
11. Add the other tablespoon of oil over the zucchinis.
12. And cook for about 20 minutes, or in any case, until golden brown.
13. After the indicated time, take it out of the oven and serve after letting it cool down for a few minutes.
14. Serve the baked ginger zucchini and the eggs pieces.

NUTRITIONAL VALUES:

CARBS	PROTEINS	FATS	CALORIES
5gr	11gr	8gr	130

SIDE DISHES RECIPES

Carrot and egg white frittata

INGREDIENTS FOR 2 SERVINGS

- 4 egg whites
- 1 big size carrot
- 1 tbsp of chopped red onion
- 1 tbsp of sugar free almond milk
- 1 tbsp of soy grated cheese
- Salt and pepper to taste.
- Olive oil to taste
- 1 pinch of turmeric powder

INGREDIENTS FOR 3 SERVINGS

- 6 egg whites
- 1 big size carrot
- 2 tbsp of chopped red onion
- 2 tbsp of sugar free almond milk
- 2 tbsp of soy grated cheese
- Salt and pepper to taste.
- Olive oil to taste
- 2 pinches of turmeric powder

PREP. TIME	COOKING TIME	DIFFICULTY	A.I. GRADE
20 minutes	30 minutes	●●●○○	Good

DIRECTIONS

1. First step of this recipe: wash and peel the big size carrot, then cut in into some slices.
2. Meanwhile, peel and fry the chopped red onion in a pan heated with olive oil.
3. As soon as the onion has browned, remove it and sauté the carrot slices for about ten minutes.
4. While the carrot slices are cooking, batter the 4 egg whites in a plate and together with the milk, pepper, turmeric powder, and salt.
5. Mix the sautéed carrots and mix well.
6. Sprinkle soy cheese and stir well.
7. Heat the olive oil in a non-stick pan.
8. Once oil is hot, pour the battered egg white with the carrots.
9. Cook for 3-4 minutes on each side, turning with a plate like a simple frittata.
10. Serve the carrot and turmeric frittata still hot.

NUTRITIONAL VALUES:

CARBS	PROTEINS	FATS	CALORIES
10gr	14gr	3gr	160

SIDE DISHES RECIPES

Smoked salmon and chia seeds eggs

INGREDIENTS FOR 2 SERVINGS

- 2 big size eggs
- 1 tsp of chia seeds
- 2 teaspoons of mustard
- 2 threads of chives
- 3 slices of smoked salmon
- Salt to taste.
- Chili pepper to taste

INGREDIENTS FOR 3 SERVINGS

- 3 big size eggs
- 1 tbsp of chia seeds
- 3 teaspoons of mustard
- 3 threads of chives
- 5 slices of smoked salmon
- Salt to taste.
- Chili pepper to taste

PREP. TIME	COOKING TIME	DIFFICULTY	A.I. GRADE
15 minutes	10 minutes	●●○○○	GOOD

DIRECTIONS

1. Start the anti-inflammatory recipe by boiling the eggs. Put a saucepan full of water and bring some water to a boil. Once boiling, arrange the eggs and cook them for 10 minutes.
2. After cooking, take the eggs out of the water and let them to cool with cold water and then peel them.
3. Split the eggs in half, remove the yolks and set them aside in a bowl.
4. So, arrange the egg whites in a serving dish.
5. Take the chives, wash them, and then chop them finely.
6. Grasp the bowl with the yolks and mash them with a fork.
7. Add the chives, a pinch of salt and the mustard and mix the ingredients with a fork until you obtain a smooth and thick sauce.
8. Put the egg yolk sauce inside each egg white.
9. Divide the smoked salmon slices in half, roll them up and then place them on top of the roe.
10. Decorate the eggs with a few chia seeds and serve.

NUTRITIONAL VALUES:

CARBS	PROTEINS	FATS	CALORIES
3gr	14gr	19gr	250

SIDE DISHES RECIPES

Spinach and tuna eggs

INGREDIENTS FOR 2 SERVINGS

- 4 small size eggs
- 1/3 cup of cooked spinach
- 1 tsp of ginger powder
- 1/3 cup of drained tuna in oil
- 1 pinch of cinnamon
- 1 tsp of olive oil
- Salt to taste
- 1 teaspoon of fresh chopped cilantro

INGREDIENTS FOR 3 SERVINGS

- 6 small size eggs
- 1/2 cup of cooked spinach
- 2 tsp of ginger powder
- 1/2 cup of drained tuna in oil
- 1 tsp of cinnamon
- 2 tsp of olive oil
- Salt to taste
- 2 tsp of fresh chopped cilantro

PREP. TIME	COOKING TIME	DIFFICULTY	A.I. GRADE
10 minutes	10 minutes	●●○○○	Good

DIRECTIONS

1. Start this recipe by draining both spinach and tuna.
2. So, grasp a non-stick pan and heat the oil.
3. Once hot, add the tuna and spinach and brown them for 3 minutes, seasoning with salt, ginger powder, and a pinch of cinnamon. Turn off.
4. Meanwhile, in a dish, batter the eggs and after they are perfectly beaten, put the eggs in the pan with spinach and tuna.
5. Stir constantly and find a way the divide the eggs in many pieces.
6. Cook for other 5 minutes and then arrange the eggs into a serving plate.
7. Wash and chop the cilantro leaves.
8. Serve the tuna and spinach omelette hot sprinkled with chopped cilantro leaves.

NUTRITIONAL VALUES:

CARBS	PROTEINS	FATS	CALORIES
7gr	32gr	14gr	300

SIDE DISHES RECIPES

Almond, carrot and red cabbage

INGREDIENTS FOR 2 SERVINGS

- 1 carrot sliced (1 cup about)
- 1 cup of red cabbage leaves
- A spoonful of apple cider vinegar
- Two sprigs of thyme
- Almond flour to taste
- Salt and pepper to taste
- Olive oil to tasteo

INGREDIENTS FOR 3 SERVINGS

- 2 carrots sliced (1 cup and ½ about)
- 1 cup and ½ of red cabbage leaves
- 1 tbsp of apple cider vinegar
- 3 sprigs of thyme
- Almond flour to taste
- Salt and pepper to taste
- Olive oil to taste

PREP. TIME	COOKING TIME	DIFFICULTY	A.I. GRADE
15 minutes	10 minutes	●●○○○	Good

DIRECTIONS

1. First, wash and pat dry the slices of carrot.
2. Season the veggie with salt and pepper.
3. Wash and dry the thyme and then chop it.
4. Put the almond flour on a plate and flour the carrot slices on both sides.
5. Heat a tablespoon of oil in a pan and cook the almond carrots for 8 minutes, turning it once.
6. Once they are cooked, take the carrots slices away from the pan and keep them on a warm plate.
7. Meanwhile, wash the red cabbage leaves and chop them.
8. Season them with oil, salt, and apple cider vinegar
9. Now put the almond carrot slices on serving plates, surround with the red cabbage salad and serve.

NUTRITIONAL VALUES:

CARBS	PROTEINS	FATS	CALORIES
12gr	2gr	9gr	70

SIDE DISHES RECIPES

Asparagus and almond soy salad

INGREDIENTS FOR 2 SERVINGS

- 1/3 cup of soy cheese
- 5 oz of asparagus
- 2 tsp of chopped almonds
- A shallot
- A sprig of rosemary
- 2 bay leaves
- 2 tsp of olive oil
- Salt and pepper to taste

INGREDIENTS FOR 3 SERVINGS

- ½ cup of soy cheese
- 7.5 oz of asparagus
- 3 tsp of chopped almonds
- 1 shallot
- 2 sprigs of rosemary
- 3 bay leaves
- 3 tsp of olive oil
- Salt and pepper to taste

PREP. TIME	COOKING TIME	DIFFICULTY	A.I. GRADE
15 minutes	15 minutes	●●○○○	GOOD

DIRECTIONS

1. First step of this recipe: trim and peel the asparagus.
2. Wash them under running water and then dry them.
3. Bring a pot of already salted water to the boil and blanch the asparagus for 8 minutes.
4. Switch off and let the asparagus drain.
5. Peel and wash the shallot and then cut it into thin slices.
6. Heat the olive oil in a pan and then brown the shallot for a couple of minutes.
7. Add the asparagus and cook for 4/5 minutes, seasoning with salt and pepper.
8. Wash and dry the bay leawes and rosemary.
9. Serve the soy cheese pieces with the asparagus, shallots, and a sprinkle of chopped almonds.

NUTRITIONAL VALUES:

CARBS	PROTEINS	FATS	CALORIES
7gr	16gr	15gr	210

SIDE DISHES RECIPES

Radicchio, avocado and cherry tomato salad

INGREDIENTS FOR 2 SERVINGS

- 5 large leaves of radicchio
- 4 cherry tomatoes
- 1/3 cup of cubed avocado
- 2 tsp of mustard
- 2 tsp of apple cider vinegar
- 1 tsp of dried oregano
- Salt and pepper to taste

INGREDIENTS FOR 3 SERVINGS

- 8 large leaves of radicchio
- 6 cherry tomatoes
- 1/2 cup of cubed avocado
- 3 tsp of mustard
- 3 tsp of apple cider vinegar
- 1 tsp of dried oregano
- Salt and pepper to taste

PREP. TIME	COOKING TIME	DIFFICULTY	A.I. GRADE
15 minutes	/	●○○○○	Top

DIRECTIONS

1. Start the recipe by peeling, washing, and drying the avocado, then cut it into small cube (1/3 cup).
2. Wash the radicchio leaves and dry them too, then split it into thin slices.
3. Wash and dry the four cherry tomatoes and then cut them in quarters.
4. Now put the avocado, chopped radicchio and cherry tomatoes in a bowl.
5. Add the apple cider vinegar, the mustard, a pinch of salt and pepper and stir everything.
6. Finish decorating the salad with dried oregano and serve.

NUTRITIONAL VALUES:

CARBS	PROTEINS	FATS	CALORIES
12gr	7gr	13gr	180

SIDE DISHES RECIPES

Baked zucchini and artichokes

INGREDIENTS FOR 2 SERVINGS

- 1 cup of zucchinis
- A lemon
- 2 artichokes
- 3 sage leaves
- Salt and pepper to taste
- Olive oil to taste

INGREDIENTS FOR 3 SERVINGS

- 1 cup and ½ of zucchinis
- A lemon
- 3 artichokes
- 5 sage leaves
- Salt and pepper to taste
- Olive oil to taste

PREP. TIME	COOKING TIME	DIFFICULTY	A.I. GRADE
15 minutes	20 minutes	●●○○○	GOOD

DIRECTIONS

1. Start this anti-inflammatory recipe with the artichokes. Remove the stem and tough leaves.
2. Halve, remove the stubble, cut them into wedges and put them to wash in a bowl with water and lemon juice.
3. Wash and dry the zucchini in the meantime, and slice them.
4. Wash the sage leaves too.
5. So, brush a pan with oil and then arrange the artichokes and zucchini slice inside of it. Season them with oil, salt and pepper, sage leaves and then cook at 400°F for 20 minutes.
6. Once cooked, serve the zucchini slices surrounded by artichokes directly on two serving plates.

NUTRITIONAL VALUES:

CARBS	PROTEINS	FATS	CALORIES
8gr	5gr	4gr	50

SIDE DISHES RECIPES

Coleslaw with mushrooms

INGREDIENTS FOR 2 SERVINGS

- 1 cup of cabbage
- 1 tsp of ginger powder
- 6 Champignon mushrooms
- 2 tsp of chia seeds
- 2 leeks
- Apple cider vinegar to taste
- Salt and pepper to taste
- Olive oil to taste

INGREDIENTS FOR 3 SERVINGS

- 1 cup and ½ of cabbage
- 2 tsp of ginger powder
- 9 Champignon mushrooms
- 3 tsp of chia seeds
- 3 leeks
- Apple cider vinegar to taste
- Salt and pepper to taste
- Olive oil to taste

PREP. TIME	COOKING TIME	DIFFICULTY	A.I. GRADE
20 minutes	10 minutes	●●●○○	Top

DIRECTIONS

1. First, wash and dry the cabbage, chop it and season with salt, ginger powder, and pepper.
2. Put it in a pan brushed with olive oil and cook in the oven at 400°F for 10 minutes.
3. Meanwhile, take away the earthy part from the mushrooms, wash them, dry them, and then cut them into thin slices.
4. Clean, trim and wash the leeks and then cut them into slices as well.
5. As soon as the cabbage is cooked, take it out of the oven and let it rest for 5 minutes.
6. Divide the sliced mushrooms and leeks between two serving plates.
7. Place the cabbage on top of the vegetables.
8. Put a spoonful of oil, two of apple cider vinegar, chia seeds, salt and pepper in a bowl and mix.
9. Sprinkle the cabbage and vegetables with the chia seeds emulsion and serve.

NUTRITIONAL VALUES:

CARBS	PROTEINS	FATS	CALORIES
5gr	10gr	6gr	90

SIDE DISHES RECIPES

Green beans and carrots tofu cheese

INGREDIENTS FOR 2 SERVINGS

- 1 cup of tofu cheese
- 2 small carrots
- ½ cup of green beans
- 2 tsp of fresh sugar free apple juice
- 1 tsp ginger powder
- 3 tsp of apple cider vinegar
- Salt and pepper to taste
- Olive oil to taste

INGREDIENTS FOR 3 SERVINGS

- 1 cup and ½ of tofu cheese
- 3 small carrots
- 1 cup of green beans
- 3 tsp of fresh sugar free apple juice
- 1 tsp ginger powder
- 5 tsp of apple cider vinegar
- Salt and pepper to taste
- Olive oil to taste

PREP. TIME	COOKING TIME	DIFFICULTY	A.I. GRADE
15 minutes	20 minutes	●●●○○	GOOD

DIRECTIONS

1. As first operation for this recipe, rinse the tofu cheese, cut it into cubes and put it in a bowl.
2. Add the apple juice, soy sauce and ginger and let it marinate for 10 minutes.
3. In the meantime, trim the green beans, wash them, and then split into 3 pieces.
4. Peel and wash the carrots and then cut them into slices.
5. After the marinating time, heat a spoonful of olive oil in a pan and, as soon as it is hot enough, put the carrots and green beans to cook for 15 minutes.
6. Now add the tofu cheese with the marinating liquid, season with salt and pepper and keep on cooking for another 5 minutes, stirring often.
7. After 5 minutes, turn off the heat and put the tofu cheese and vegetables on serving plates.
8. Sprinkle with the apple juice cooking liquid and serve.

NUTRITIONAL VALUES:

CARBS	PROTEINS	FATS	CALORIES
13gr	15gr	8gr	180

SIDE DISHES RECIPES

Seeds and nuts stuffed avocado

INGREDIENTS FOR 2 SERVINGS

- 1 ripe avocado
- 2 tsp of chopped walnuts
- 2 tsp of chopped hazelnuts
- 2 tsp of chia seeds
- 1 ripe tomato
- ½ lime
- 1 tsp of soy sauce
- Salt and pepper to taste
- Olive oil to taste

INGREDIENTS FOR 3 SERVINGS

- 2 small size ripe avocado
- 3 tsp of chopped walnuts
- 3 tsp of chopped hazelnuts
- 3 tsp of chia seeds
- 1 ripe tomato
- 1 lime
- 2 tsp of soy sauce
- Salt and pepper to taste
- Olive oil to taste

PREP. TIME	COOKING TIME	DIFFICULTY	A.I. GRADE
15 minutes	/	●●○○○	GOOD

DIRECTIONS

1. As first step for this recipe: wash and dry the avocado, halve, and pit.
2. Take the out the pulp of it with the help of a spoon and put it in a bowl.
3. Wash the ripe tomato, slit into cubes, and put it in the bowl with the avocado pulp.
4. Join the lime juice to the avocado, and add seeds, nuts, salt, pepper, soy sauce and a little oil too. Stir and mix well.
5. Put the halved avocado on two dished and add the filling. After you have fillet both the halves, serve this anti-inflammatory side dish.

NUTRITIONAL VALUES:

CARBS	PROTEINS	FATS	CALORIES
5gr	8gr	22gr	280

SIDE DISHES RECIPES

Soy cheese and hazelnuts cucumber rolls

INGREDIENTS FOR 2 SERVINGS

- 4 cucumber slices
- ½ cup of soy cheese
- 1 tbsp of hazelnuts
- ¼ cup of salad leaves
- 2 tsp of Olive oil
- Salt and pepper to taste

INGREDIENTS FOR 3 SERVINGS

- 6 cucumber slices
- 1 cup of soy cheese
- 2 tbsp of hazelnuts
- 1 cup of salad leaves
- 3 tsp of Olive oil
- Salt and pepper to taste

PREP. TIME	COOKING TIME	DIFFICULTY	A.I. GRADE
10 minutes + 40 minutes to rest in the fridge	/	●●○○○	Top

DIRECTIONS

1. First, take a bowl (or a deep plate) and put the soy cheese inside.
2. Flavor it with a spoonful of olive oil, salt, and pepper.
3. Finely chop the hazelnuts and then add them to the soy cheese. Mix everything with a fork.
4. Now take the cucumber slices and fill them with the soy cheese mixture and add a little salad to each slice.
5. Close the cucumber rolls carefully and put them in the fridge to rest for 30/40 minutes before serving.
6. Serve it all as a snack.

NUTRITIONAL VALUES:

CARBS	PROTEINS	FATS	CALORIES
5gr	10gr	8gr	130

SIDE DISHES RECIPES

Turmeric and coconut spinach

INGREDIENTS
FOR 2 SERVINGS

- 1 cup and ½ of fresh spinach
- 2 tbsp of lime juice
- 2 tbsp of coconut milk
- 2 tsp olive oil
- 1 tsp of turmeric powder
- Salt and pepper to taste

INGREDIENTS
FOR 3 SERVINGS

- 2 cups of fresh spinach
- 3 tbsp of lime juice
- 3 tbsp of coconut milk
- 3 tsp olive oil
- 1 tsp of turmeric powder
- Salt and pepper to taste

PREP. TIME	COOKING TIME	DIFFICULTY	A.I. GRADE
10 minutes	20 minutes	●●○○○	GOOD

DIRECTIONS

1. First step for this anti-inflammatory side dish: rinse the fresh spinach leaves under running water and steam them.
2. Cook them for about ten minutes, just long enough to let them dry.
3. Meanwhile, heat a non-stick pan with a little oil.
4. Add the spinach, a pinch of salt and a pinch of pepper.
5. Pour in the lime juice and coconut milk, so cook for a few minutes.
6. After 3 minutes, you can add the turmeric powder.
7. Stir until the turmeric powder is completely incorporated.
8. Serve the spinach with turmeric while are still hot directly on serving plates.

NUTRITIONAL VALUES:

CARBS	PROTEINS	FATS	CALORIES
3gr	6gr	8gr	80

28 days Meal Plan

DAY 1

Breakfast:	1 glass of citrus juice + 2 avocado toasts
Snack:	1 kiwi and 2 walnuts
Lunch:	4.9 oz of turmeric chicken rice with 7 oz of spinach
Snack:	1 smoothie and 1 tbsp of almonds
Dinner:	5.2 oz of beef steak with tomatoes and oregano, 7 oz of fennel
Total:	**1350 kcal**

DAY 2

Breakfast:	an apple, whole grain rusks with sugar-free jam and a cup of tea
Snack:	a glass of citrus fruit juice and 2 walnuts
Lunch:	7 oz of baked sea bass topped with lemon and parsley, 7 oz of broccoli
Snack:	1 cup of apple puree with rolled oats and flaked almonds
Dinner:	4.9 oz of bean soup and 7 oz of grilled salmon
Total:	**1350 kcal**

DAY 3

Breakfast:	1 glass of blueberry juice, two whole grain rusks and a teaspoon of honey
Snack:	½ cup of rice yogurt, 3.5 oz of red fruits of your choice and a few squares of dark chocolate, minimum 70% cocoa
Lunch:	4.9 oz of whole wheat pasta, 1 boiled egg, 1 mixed salad
Snack:	1 banana smoothie with almond milk
Dinner:	4.9 oz brown rice with zucchini, tuna, and avocado, 7 oz grilled peppers
Total:	**1350 kcal**

DAY 4

Breakfast:	A pear, ½ cup of rice yogurt with rolled oats and bran sticks and a cup of tea
Snack:	1 glass of grapefruit juice and 5 almonds
Lunch:	7 oz of fresh tuna, 7 oz of zucchinis and 2 whole grain rusks
Snack:	2 apples
Dinner:	7 oz of baked cod, radishes, and 7 oz of mushrooms cucumber salad
Total:	**1350 kcal**

DAY 5

Breakfast:	1 glass of sugar free vegetable milk, 3 whole grain rusks, 3 tsp of jam with no added sugar
Snack:	5.2 oz of pineapple
Lunch:	5.2 oz of baked chicken breast, lettuce + tomato salad, 1 whole grain bun of 1 oz
Snack:	2 kiwis
Dinner:	7 oz of zucchini and avocado turmeric salmon, 7 oz of green salad, 1 oz of whole grain bun
Total:	**1350 kcal**

DAY 6

Breakfast:	1/2 cup of Greek yogurt, 3 whole grain biscuits, 1 orange
Snack:	2 peaches
Lunch:	7 oz of steamed sage and ginger halibut, 7 oz of grilled zucchini
Snack:	2 pears
Dinner:	7 oz of cream of pumpkin and shrimps, avocado and cherry tomato stuffed radicchio
Total:	**1350 kcal**

DAY 7

Breakfast:	1 banana porridge
Snack:	1 apple, kiwi, and cucumber smoothie
Lunch:	4.9 oz of tomato lentil soup, 5.2 oz of grilled tuna
Snack:	1 carrot centrifuge
Dinner:	7 oz of apple and ginger sea bream fillets, 7 oz of green salad
Total:	**1350 kcal**

DAY 8

Breakfast:	2 salmon toast, 1 cup of green tea
Snack:	1 banana
Lunch:	4.9 oz of spaghetti with shrimps and cherry tomatoes, 5.2 oz of grilled tuna
Snack:	detox cocktail
Dinner:	7 oz of mushroom cream plaice fillet, 1 oz whole grain bun
Total:	**1350 kcal**

DAY 9

Breakfast:	1/2 cup of Greek yogurt, 1 glass of orange juice
Snack:	5.2 oz of melon
Lunch:	4.9 oz of whole wheat spaghetti with lemon, 7 oz of almond and spice breaded cod
Snack:	2 pears
Dinner:	7 oz of coconut milk and beets green salmon and 1 oz whole grain bun
Total:	**1350 kcal**

DAY 10

Breakfast:	1 apple porridge, 2 whole grain biscuits
Snack:	1 cucumber smoothie
Lunch:	4.9 oz of pasta salad with avocado and tuna, 1 green salad
Snack:	2 apricots
Dinner:	7 oz of tangerine and pineapple cod, 7 oz of green beans, and carrots cream cheese
Total:	**1350 kcal**

Anti Inflammatory

DAY 11

Breakfast:	1 cup of sugar-free almond milk
Snack:	1 kiwi, grapefruit, and papaya smoothie
Lunch:	5.2 oz of cream of beans and shrimps, 5.2 oz of grilled cod
Snack:	½ cup of Greek yogurt and 5 almonds
Dinner:	7 oz of apple and ginger sea bream fillets, 7 oz of cherry tomatoes salad, 1 oz whole-grain bun
Total:	**1350 kcal**

DAY 12

Breakfast:	scrambled eggs with salmon, 1 glass of grapefruit juice
Snack:	1 watermelon, strawberry, and cherry smoothie
Lunch:	4.9 oz of black rice with avocado and crabmeat, 7 oz of grilled zucchini
Snack:	1 frozen yogurt with cherries
Dinner:	7 oz of cauliflower chia seeds and ginger chicken, 7 oz of baked zucchini and artichokes
Total:	**1350 kcal**

DAY 13

Breakfast:	2 salmon toast, 1 cup of green tea
Snack:	2 pears
Lunch:	7 oz of basil pistachio and turmeric mackerel, 7 oz of grilled peppers
Snack:	2 peaches
Dinner:	baked ginger zucchini eggs and soy cheese, 1 oz of whole-grain bun, 1 green salad
Total:	**1350 kcal**

DAY 14

Breakfast:	1 avocado and raspberry toast, 1 glass of orange juice
Snack:	1 cup of masala chai and 6 almonds
Lunch:	4.9 oz of black rice with salmon, 7 oz of grilled zucchini
Snack:	1 whole-grain sandwich with turkey
Dinner:	herbs and melon sauce chicken cubes, 1 oz whole-grain bun
Total:	**1350 kcal**

DAY 15

Breakfast:	1 glass of citrus juice + 2 avocado toasts
Snack:	2 apples
Lunch:	4.9 oz of black rice with chicken and vegetables, 1 green salad
Snack:	3.5 oz of strawberries
Dinner:	7 oz of saffron leek cream, 7 oz of grilled tuna
Total:	**1350 kcal**

DAY 16

Breakfast:	1 berry porridge, 3.5 oz of strawberries
Snack:	carrot centrifuge
Lunch:	4.9 oz of brown rice with chicken and mint, 7 oz of baked zucchini and artichokes
Snack:	½ cup of Greek yogurt and 3 walnuts
Dinner:	5.2 oz of sweet and sour turkey with asparagus, 1 oz of whole-grain bun
Total:	**1350 kcal**

DAY 17

Breakfast:	1 glass of blueberry juice, two whole-grain rusks and a teaspoon of honey
Snack:	2 apples
Lunch:	4.9 oz of brown rice with zucchini, tuna, and avocado, 5.2 oz of almonds carrot and red cabbage
Snack:	2 kiwis
Dinner:	smoked salmon and chia seeds eggs, 7 oz of coleslaw with mushrooms and mustard, 1 oz of whole-grain bun
Total:	**1350 kcal**

DAY 18

Breakfast:	scrambled eggs with salmon, 1 glass of orange juice
Snack:	1 apple, kiwi, and cucumber smoothie
Lunch:	4.9 oz of pasta salad with green bean cream, 5.2 oz of herbs and melon sauce chicken cubes
Snack:	2 oranges
Dinner:	7 oz of pineapple turmeric and star anise sea bream, 7 oz of grilled zucchinis
Total:	**1350 kcal**

DAY 19

Breakfast:	1 yogurt with fruit and cereals, 1 cup of green tea
Snack:	1 watermelon, strawberry, and cherry smoothie
Lunch:	1 buddha bowl with black rice and chicken, 7 oz of grilled peppers
Snack:	2 kiwis
Dinner:	7 oz of apple and ginger sea bream fillets, 7 oz of soy cheese asparagus and almond salad
Total:	**1350 kcal**

DAY 20

Breakfast:	yogurt with peaches and whole meal biscuits
Snack:	1 cucumber smoothie
Lunch:	5.2 oz of carrot, spring onion and ginger cream, 7 oz of broccoli jalapeno tilapia
Snack:	2 pears
Dinner:	lettuce and tofu salmon salad, 1.7 oz of whole-grain bun
Total:	**1350 kcal**

DAY 21

Breakfast:	1 glass of sugar free vegetable milk, 3 whole-grain rusks, 3 tsp of jam with no added sugar
Snack:	2 peaches
Lunch:	4.9 oz of whole-wheat pasta with peppers, 7 oz of grilled cod
Snack:	3.5 oz of strawberries
Dinner:	7 oz of chicken and veggies taste salad, 1.7 oz of whole-grain bun
Total:	**1350 kcal**

DAY 22

Breakfast:	scrambled eggs with herbs, 3.5 oz of berries
Snack:	3.5 oz of blueberries
Lunch:	cream of beans, salmon, and celery, 1.7 oz of whole-grain bun
Snack:	1 detox cocktail, 2 peaches
Dinner:	7 oz of garlic and pistachio turkey legs, 1 radishes and mushrooms cucumber salad
Total:	**1350 kcal**

DAY 23

Breakfast:	2 salmon toast, 1 glass of pineapple juice
Snack:	frozen yogurt with cherries, 5 almonds
Lunch:	coconut milk and beets green salmon, 7 oz of green salad
Snack:	3.5 oz of strawberries
Dinner:	5 oz of tomato porridge, 7 oz of ginger and jalapeno baked tuna
Total:	**1350 kcal**

DAY 24

Breakfast:	scrambled eggs with salmon, 1 glass of grapefruit juice
Snack:	½ cup of Greek yogurt, 3 walnuts
Lunch:	smoked salmon and chia seeds eggs, 7 oz of turmeric and coconut spinach
Snack:	watermelon, strawberry, and cherry smoothie
Dinner:	poke bowl with shrimps, 7 oz of grilled vegetables
Total:	**1350 kcal**

DAY 25

Breakfast:	yogurt with peaches and whole-grain biscuits, 1 cup of green tea
Snack:	2 apricots
Lunch:	4.9 oz of rice with spinach and salmon, 7 oz of tomatoes and green beans salad
Snack:	masala chai, 3 whole-grain rusks
Dinner:	7 oz of green beans and honey salmon, 1,7 of rye bread
Total:	**1350 kcal**

DAY 26

Breakfast:	yogurt with fruit and cereals, 1 glass of grapefruit juice
Snack:	1 whole-grain sandwich with turkey
Lunch:	cream of broad beans and peas, 7 oz of orange and avocado halibut
Snack:	3.5 oz of blackberries
Dinner:	7 oz of tangerine and pineapple cod, 7 oz of almonds carrot and red cabbage
Total:	**1350 kcal**

DAY 27

Breakfast:	1 avocado and raspberry toast, 1 glass of orange juice
Snack:	3.5 oz of raspberries
Lunch:	7 oz of cream of pumpkin and mushrooms, carrot, and egg white frittata
Snack:	1 kiwi, grapefruit, and papaya smoothie
Dinner:	7 oz of orange turkey and veggies, 1.7 oz of whole-grain bread
Total:	**1350 kcal**

DAY 28

Breakfast:	scrambled eggs with salmon, 1 glass of pineapple juice
Snack:	1 apple and 5 almonds
Lunch:	mushroom and hazelnut soup, 7 oz of tilapia with lime and pecans
Snack:	1 watermelon, strawberry, and cherry smoothie
Dinner:	7 oz of mushroom cream plaice fillet, 7 oz of green salad, 1 oz of whole-grain bun
Total:	**1350 kcal**

Printed in Great Britain
by Amazon